CORPORATE LONGITUDE

What you need to know to navigate the knowledge economy

Leif Edvinsson

FINANCIAL TIMES
Prentice Hall

An imprint of **Pearson Education**

London · New York · Toronto · Sydney · Tokyo · Singapore · Hong Kong · Cape Town
New Delhi · Madrid · Paris · Amsterdam · Munich · Milan · Stockholm

PEARSON EDUCATION LIMITED

Head Office:
Edinburgh Gate
Harlow CM20 2JE
Tel: +44 (0)1279 623623
Fax: +44 (0)1279 431059

London Office:
128 Long Acre
London WC2E 9AN
Tel: +44 (0)20 7447 2000
Fax: +44 (0)20 7240 5771
Website: www.business-minds.com

First published in Great Britain in 2002
First published in Sweden in 2002 by BookHouse Publishing

© BookHouse Publishing 2002

The right of Leif Edvinsson to be identified as Author
of this Work has been asserted by him in accordance
with the Copyright, Designs and Patents Act 1988.

ISBN 0 273 65627 9

British Library Cataloguing in Publication Data
A CIP catalogue record for this book can be obtained from the British Library

10 9 8 7 6 5 4 3 2 1

Typeset by Pantek Arts Ltd, Maidstone
Printed and bound in Great Britain by Biddles Ltd, Guildford & Kings Lynn

The Publishers' policy is to use paper manufactured from sustainable forests.

CONTENTS

ABOUT THE AUTHOR

Global knowledge nomad Leif Edvinsson championed early moves to nourish intellectual capital (IC) and to have it measured in corporate annual reports. His 1997 book, *Intellectual Capital* (co-authored with Michael Malone), drew on Edvinsson's experiences at the financial services company Skandia where he was appointed the world's first corporate director of intellectual capital in 1991. He is also co-author of *Accounting for Minds* (with Gottfried Grafström, 1998).

At Skandia, Edvinsson pioneered the development of a management and reporting model – entitled the Navigator – based around intellectual capital. He also developed a knowledge innovation tool: the Skandia Future Center. At the beginning of 2000, it was calculated that the value of Skandia's intellectual capital was in excess of $15 billion. In 1998 he was named Brain of the Year by the Brain Trust in the UK for his pioneering work.

Having left Skandia in autumn 1999, Edvinsson was recently appointed the world's first associate professor in intellectual capital and knowledge economics at Lund University, and he is much in demand as a board member and speaker. He is now developing a chain of arenas – entitled Future Centers – to encourage insights into intellectual capital and to nurture its growth; as well as a holding company for intellectual capital recipes, Universal Networking Intellectual Capital (UNIC – www.unic.net).

> "My aim here is not to teach the method that everyone ought to follow in order to conduct his reason well, but solely to reveal how I have tried to conduct my own."
>
> **René Descartes** Discours de la méthode, 1637

THE JOURNEY

It is wise to have some idea of where you are going. In the knowledge economy it is equally important to be prepared to change direction at a moment's notice. Look at the impact of September 11, 2001. "What the events of September 11 did was to introduce a whole new set of uncertainties which information technology is not going to improve our insights into," said Federal Reserve Chairman Allan Greenspan in October 2001.

Our journey in Corporate Longitude has a number of important markers. The first is that I believe there is a new commercial reality – knowledge economics – which transforms the concept of value and of value creation. Intangibles, such as intellectual capital (in all of its manifestations), brands, trust and networks, are the driving force of knowledge economics. Organizations need to create knowledge recipes – potent combinations of tacit and implicit knowledge – if they are to succeed and develop sustainable earnings.

The rise of knowledge economics highlights a growing mismatch between current financial reporting systems and intellectual assets – these I see as similar to corporate latitude and corporate longitude. One without the other gets us nowhere.

There is a need, therefore, for new insights, models, measures, and metaphors which will allow us to capitalize on the new reality. We have to seek out fresh ways of seeing things, different perspectives, perspectives which embrace the past, present and future. We must ask questions rather than relying on answers. In the question lies our quest.

This has implications for the way companies are organized. Work, and notions of what is value creating work, have to be redefined. We must seek out new ways of organizing ourselves and our organizations. We have to move away from industrial organizations to, what I call, intelligent enterprising, inspired by the human brain and the organic world rather than machinery.

Intelligent enterprising will be bound together by three types of intelligence quotients: rational intelligence, IQ; emotional intelligence, EQ; and spiritual or synapse intelligence, SQ. Intelligent enterprising has to be built in contexts which foster and nurture creativity and imagination as well as the creation of real and long lasting meaning. The most useful imagery to describe intelligent enterprising may come from an analogy with bacteria which are mutating faster than the pharmaceutical industry can develop new recipes. Intelligent enterprising is based on feedback loops which enable rapid learning and the creation of new opportunity spaces.

All of these developments put far greater onus than ever before on individuals. You have new responsibilities to yourself and for yourself. This might be called i-commerce.

In turn, this creates new possibilities, challenges and spaces for the interface between individuals and organizations. Working together, people and organizations must blend and remix knowledge in innovative ways. This demands a new dimension to leadership – the entrepreneurial knowledge leader.

And the final destination? Organizations mutated within knowledge societies; true communities of knowledge at a personal, local, national and global level.

ACKNOWLEDGEMENTS

I would like to express my great gratitude to all my friends in the IC community and to my knowledge sharing and mind stretching friends for making this journey possible for me personally and for the benefit of my daughters, Marie and Sophie, and coming generations.

I would also like to thank Stuart Crainer and Des Dearlove of Suntop Media for their editorial help in the creation of this book. They have shared my journey.

DEPARTURE

In 1675 King Charles II of England set up the Royal Observatory – "A small observatory within Our Park at Greenwich" – on the River Thames. It was not some majestic whim or grand gesture. The Observatory was tasked with finding a method of accurately determining longitude at sea so that sailors could navigate the world's oceans.

A similar challenge currently faces the business world. Modern corporations habitually calibrate along one, single measure: financial capital. This is corporate latitude, the world of, so-called, tangible assets made up of a pile of assets built upon the famous bottom-line. The trouble is that this measure gives corporations only part of the picture, only half of the co-ordinates required to know their precise location and to map out the route to their renewal. Without another lateral co-ordinate – a measurement for intellectual capital and other vital intangibles – companies are unable to locate their true potential or chart a meaningful course into the future.

The longitude story is instructive. Despite the King's largesse and the appointment of an Astronomer Royal, answers did not immediately emerge. In characteristic organizational fashion, the British Government decided to throw money at the problem – the then massive sum of £20,000 was offered for a solution "tried and found Practicable and Useful at Sea" which could provide longitude to within half-a-degree. Equally characteristically, the Government set up a committee, the Board of Longitude.

For a while "Finding the longitude" attracted every weird, eccentric, money-grabbing, inventor in Europe. In Britain at the time, astronomy was something of a national pasttime. The Observatory's architect Sir Christopher Wren was also a part-time astronomer. The cause was celebrated, akin to the modern splitting of the atom. It was thought that the answer to the problem would emerge, in time, from the scientific elite or the professionals in the Navy. Meanwhile the Board of Longitude dealt with a series of bizarre perpetual motion machines and suggestions on how to square circles.

Then, in 1735, a little-educated clockmaker from Lincolnshire arrived in London with a marine timekeeper – the precursor of the chronometer. The unknown upstart was John Harrison. Harrison was an intellectual, professional and knowledge outsider. He was also an inspired thinker and innovator. But the power of prejudice and blinkered ignorance was to work against his brilliance. He was ignored and overlooked.

In fact, it took the next thirty years for Harrison to enhance his design and to convince the highly sceptical Board of Longitude that he possessed the answer and deserved the prize. Indeed, having received half the prize money, Harrison only received additional payment when he petitioned the King and Parliament. It was not until 1773 that John Harrison was recognized as the solver of the longitude conundrum. Not until 1884 did longitude become the global standard as the Greenwich Meridian (and only in 1921 did the world introduce universal time).

Today, you can stand astride the Greenwich Meridian Line, one foot in the Eastern hemisphere, the other in the West. It is one of those experiences which means so little and yet signifies so much. Follow the line for two and a half kilometres northwards and you reach the Millennium Dome.

Once inside the cavernous Dome, one of the millennium year exhibition's highlights was a massive human body. For the purposes of edutainment, the brain was a cavernous hole filled with tapes of an old-fashioned British comedian and decorated with numerous of the comedian's trademark fez. Standing in the brain in much the same way as I stood astride the Meridian Line, it looked so important, yet so trivial. Answers were there but somehow they were out of reach. Even in the neon-lit, all-explaining world of edutainment, the brain remains a misunderstood place.

The blanket of ignorance, or emptiness, surrounding the human mind mirrors the disbelief encountered by John Harrison over three hundred years ago. To most twenty-first-century men and women, the mind is as mysterious as longitude was to eighteenth-century sailors. Even now, news of what the mind can do and how it can work is usually greeted with cynical disbelief.

We are disbelieving of the brain's potential. Perhaps we are fearful of where that may lead. The reality is that we do not know our way around our own minds. We need fresh, longitudinal, perspectives to make sense of our most cherished possession.

At an organizational level the implications are also significant. The modern organization is a complex networked organism, equipped from top to bottom with the latest in modern technology. It gives the appearance of being incredibly sophisticated. Urbane, smooth young executives jet around the world armed with their laptops, mobile phones, electronic organizers. They interact in different locations, criss-crossing cultures and time zones with something approaching abandon. They are, in the words of John Micklethwait and Adrian Wooldrige in their book *A Future Perfect*, "cosmocrats", the new glittering stars in the corporate firmament.

Yet, faced with an intractable problem such as corporate longitude, cosmocrats are as likely to set up a committee – now renamed a project team – and offer a reward for a solution (usually in the form of share options rather than old-fashioned cash) as was the British Government of the eighteenth century. Only time moves on; managerial methods and notions of how best to organize ourselves often stand resolutely still resulting in institutional failures. As the world moves on our perceptions are static.

However, the most telling comparison between the quest to make sense of longitude and the modern corporate world lies in the notion of measurement. Sailors needed a clockmaker to crack the longitude problem so they could chart their whereabouts accurately and easily. Working with latitude alone only gets you so far.

Indeed, without means of measuring longitude all navigation was regional. Chinese sailors could not navigate in Micronesia, Polynesians could not reach South America, Indian Ocean sailors could not pass the Mozambique channel, and Europeans – including the Vikings – remained mainly coastal navigators. Traditional navigators all knew how to sail in bounded regions, but few could sail beyond their own locale with precision.

And this is the context in which modern corporations and institutions operate. For all the talk of the global economy, companies and those who work within them remain trapped in their own intellectual and geographical locale. They are fearful of leaving the protection of the coastal shelf and the winds they know. They need the reassurance of their familiar coast in the distance. To move further out, to venture from safety into new realms filled with personal and commercial potential, they need the corporate incarnation of John Harrison to make an appearance. A practicable method for measuring corporate longitude is urgently needed.

Corporate Longitude describes my approach to this huge problem for the world's organizations. It does not provide a definitive compass for our organizational and personal behavior. Instead, I hope, *Corporate Longitude* offers different ways of looking at problems; new questions. I believe that it is only through new questions and perspectives that we can gain new insights. As Albert Einstein put it: "The mere formulation of a problem is far more essential than its solution, which may be merely a matter of mathematical or experimental skills. To raise new questions, new possibilities, to regard old problems from a new angle requires creative imagination and marks real advances in science."

It is only through new questions and perspectives that we will be able to chart the uncertain waters of our futures. The future, after all, is made up of what we do not know. Join me in a knowledge navigation journey, exploring the futures of the mind and of knowledge enterprising.

Leif Edvinsson,
March 2002

My Journey

Every journey begins but not all reach their aspired end.

THE SMELL OF TAR

If you drive out of Stockholm for about 35 minutes you will eventually arrive at the picturesque seaside town of Vaxholm. Better still is to take one of the boats, which leave from outside the Grand Hotel in the middle of the city, and wend your way around the islands of the archipelago before reaching the town. Vaxholm has the air of a New England fishing village. It is small and quiet. The air is clean. During the summer you can sit and idly contemplate the boats nipping between the islands of the archipelago. It is a restful place.

By the Rindö ferry, right on the seashore, is a neatly kept, unassuming traditional wooden building, the Villa Askudden. Built in 1860 it was once a hotel. You can imagine genteel Victorians sitting there gazing out to sea.

Today, the Villa Askudden has been reinvented as the Skandia Future Center though it is in no way futuristic in design or appearance. It is an IC (Intellectual Capital) arena for which I was a conceptual architect (together with the world's very first IC cultivator Ingrid Tidhult).[1] Buildings have conceptual foundations as well as cement ones. The Center resonates with meaning as soon as you step over the threshold. Architecture and the contextual environment have an impact on our lives and our thinking.[2]

Let me take you there.

Through the door, there is a smell which people often struggle to place. They know they recognize it, but aren't quite sure what it can be. In fact, it is tar. The floors are sealed with tar to produce the authentic smell of a ship. The thick ropes, which rise by the winding staircase, too, are soaked in tar. There is something elemental about the smell. It reminds people of tar-covered boats. Even though I suspect that very few professional sailors now walk through the Villa's doors, at a subliminal level the smell of tar connects. Elsewhere there are the smells of cinnamon and vanilla. Vanilla is associated with creativity. Cinnamon is the essence of kitchens; homely, nourishing, nurturing. It stimulates a feeling of belonging.

Indeed, the kitchen is central to the experience. The kitchen is the reception area, the heart and focal point of the Villa – as it is in anyone's home. It is a space for knowledge exchange. It's here, after all, where you find warmth, friendship and delicious aromas. Good food and stimulating talk are essential to releasing potential thoughts and feelings.

Journey around the Villa and you find yourself in different environments. Different rooms and open-air areas of various kinds and sizes allow many forms of meeting. Rooms have different names – the Space Lab, the Navigator and so on – and different ambiences. You feel differently in different rooms, amid different things, colors and decorations. After all, different meetings require different contexts and spaces. Some people respond more creatively in a different sort of environment. One man's comfort zone is another's prison.

It is not that each room has had some dramatic make over – there is not a black room nor a high-tech room. All the rooms have the same simple but distinctive carpentry, which the house would have had when first built. Environments are created in different ways. As every lover knows, music sets the tone. So, there are five different music channels. Switch on traditional Swedish sea shanties and you create quite a different atmosphere than if you select jazz saxophonist Jan Garbarek or even Shania Twain. Similarly, different types of seating create different situations and environments. Furniture can dictate the atmosphere of any meeting – think of its effect on our body language. There are room dividers styled like sails, which can subtly separate spaces. There are different styles in different spaces. Comfortable heavily cushioned chairs, modern triumphs of scant minimalism, oaken tables, decorated table and so on. The variations are endless and endlessly stimulating.

Around the building there are historical artifacts. In one of the main meeting rooms, a ship's wheel and antique compass have pride of place. They signify a central theme of my work. These were not bought en masse from some providers of the historical Swedish nautical look. It is not a theme bar. Instead we have the old sextant from a ship. Marked with the maker's name – Whyte and Thompson, Glasgow – it is a thing of beauty. As you stand there, looking through the window out to sea, it is almost as if the entire building is an ancient wooden boat, moving with the relentless swell of the sea. You feel as though you are in charge, piloting your way through treacherous waters.

The image is deliberate. What if you were piloting a corporate ship? Which dials would you pay attention to? How would you maximize the potential of your crew and decide on a destination?

Elsewhere in the Villa, there is an old filing cabinet and an antique ledger. Mere artifacts, but they resonate with meaning. Our PCs still use the language and data management techniques of the filing cabinet. The word "file" still means much the same whether we're talking about a computer file or a paper one. Even now, in the technological age, the key book of accounting is the ledger though it is now on our screens. (The analogy can be developed still further in Swedish in which "ledger" means "to lie" due to its heavy weight.) The past sheds light – even now.

Villa Askudden is a kind of organizational laboratory for intellectual capital. Relaxed, aesthetically pleasing and comfortable, it is a prototype of future working life. It tries to optimize the opportunities for creative dialogue and knowledge sharing. It appeals to all of our senses. In many ways it is a salon rather than an office. It is a place where new ideas are born so that the world can be changed, where dialogue is a tool for value-creating renewal. In a small way it is a twenty-first century version of the colonnades of ancient Athens, the palaces of renaissance Italy and the salons of Vienna at the turn of the nineteenth century. It is a place of discovery, an arena for the cultivation of intellectual capital.

COMPASS LINKS
www.skandiafuturecenter.com
www.tidhult.com

TAKING BEARINGS
- How do you build an intellectually cultivating environment for yourself and the people you work with?
- How many different environments are there in your workplace?
- What is the rhythm and tone of your working environment?
- What is the smell of your workspace?
- Who is in charge of the cultivation of your work space?

INTELLECTUAL FUTURES

At this point, the sceptics and cynics among you will be shuffling a little uneasily. With its feng shui, lack of buzzing hardware and whirring air con, the Villa Askudden is not to everyone's taste. It is not a concrete tower block with a reassuringly large atrium, meaningless muzak, artificial plants and smiling reception team. Some may regard it as an indulgence, one of those comfortable shrines to executive privilege in which senior executives sit around and talk about strategy and the big picture.

Not so. The Villa Askudden is the embodiment of the tools for the work I undertook during eight years as director of intellectual capital at the global financial service company Skandia, which has its origins in Sweden.

Every journey has a beginning. Mine became tangible in 1991 when I became the world's first director of intellectual capital. The timing was good. In September 1991 *Fortune* published a cover picture of the left and right sides of the brain. The heading was "Brain power." "It was the first time a magazine had used a brain as the front cover," recounts the author and thinker Tony Buzan whose work has had a great deal of influence on my own perspectives. "I started collecting magazine covers featuring the brain and now have over 150 covers. The brain has become a way to sell magazines. The *Fortune* article by Thomas Stewart was the first sensible article in a business magazine about the fundamental worth of a worker and recognition of what a worker does. It has taken another ten years for it to become generic. And that's fast." [3]

Over the next eight years I worked with Skandia in developing a coherent, practical and commercially powerful means of looking at the issue of intellectual capital. You can forget the feng shui if you wish and concentrate on the bottom-line benefits to the company. They were many.

In the early 1990s the intellectual capital within Skandia had a meager value. The knowledge and expertise within the company was unco-ordinated, misunderstood and mismanaged. As a result, it was largely worthless or unvalued. Of course, there was knowledge, insight and experience in abundance, in an organization founded in 1855 and with some 10,000 people, but they simply weren't captured or used by the company in powerful, value adding ways. The potential was hidden, the value undiscovered and unacknowledged. By the beginning of 2000, the company's intellectual capital was calculated to be worth some US$15 billion. Along the way the average start-up time of new businesses within Skandia had been cut from seven years to six months.

Little wonder then that the former Skandia CEO Björn Wolrath observed in 1991: "Our intellectual capital is at least as important as our financial capital is in providing truly sustainable earnings."

And Skandia is not alone in recording such growth in its intellectual capital. Paul Strassmann has examined the performance of Abbott Laboratories. In 1991 he calculated that its net income was $1,088 million with financial capital of $3,202 million and, what Strassmann calls, "knowledge capital" of $8,209 million. By 1998 Strassmann found that the company's net income was $2,333 million with financial capital of $5,713 million. But while its financial capital and net income had grown relatively slowly over the decade, its knowledge capital had expanded rapidly. In 1998 it amounted to $39,503 million.[4]

> **Our intellectual capital is at least as important as our financial capital is in providing truly sustainable earnings.**

Professor Baruch Lev at New York's Stern University is one of the world's most widely acknowledged pioneers in the area of intellectual capital. He has compiled a lengthy list of companies with, according to his model, high knowledge capital.[5]

Knowledge works. It has to. What else is there? Every innovation starts with these intangibles.

Similarly, Tony Buzan can point to a long list of companies, which have benefited from his insights on leveraging the brain's potential:

"One of the most memorable examples was the accounts department of IBM in New York. They structured their activities through mind maps. This saved the company millions of dollars and made them money. They trained their people how to think.

"At another company all the departments mind-mapped their functions and then looked at strengths, weaknesses, needs and opinions of the other departments. Then they were all brought together and looked at the mind map and saw opportunities for synergy, for joint handling of some projects and sharing of responsibilities. In some areas a 10 percent rate of errors was reduced to 0.5 percent. The time taken to complete certain tasks was reduced from 10 hours to two.

"One organization I have worked with is the Liechtenstein Global Trust, which is a $50 billion bank with about 1000 people. Half of them have now been trained – an average of four weeks each. The training covers the mind and the body – they're taught about mind mapping; innovation; creativity; knowledge management; communication skills; poetry to strengthen their metaphorical muscle; aerobic fitness; Aikido; rowing; and mind sports like chess and goh. This has transformed the company's culture, personal and family lives. People are healthier and communications skills have been notably enhanced."[6]

Giving people the opportunity to experience new ideas works no matter what the organization. What surprises people about Skandia is that it is not in a world changing high-tech business. Nor is it located in Silicon Valley. It was just an insurance company founded in the middle of the nineteenth century in a building next to Stockholm's Royal Palace. Now it has been transformed into a global financial services company under the leadership of innovative entrepreneur Jan R. Carendi.

Intellectual capital is just as important for traditional businesses as for new economy Wunderkinder creating patents and intellectual property. It is the future of all business – literally. It is the only meaningful way to gauge the potential energy of a company. No innovation will ever take place without investment in intangibles.

Yet, as I write this book, a number of clarifications and distinctions are being made on the entire notion of intellectual capital. These are based on a number of misunderstandings.

First, people see knowledge management initiatives bite the dust and mistake knowledge management for intellectual capital. The reality is that knowledge management is only a fraction of intellectual capital. Knowledge management is about the storage, transfer and migration of knowledge. It treats knowledge as an object, like a book in a library. Intellectual capital is concerned with the future earnings potential of the organization. It is about the flow rather than the stock.[7]

The second misunderstanding is that intellectual capital simply puts a price on a company's staff. It labels them "human capital" and puts a price on their heads. This is still a common reaction from people – a major proportion of people. They see intellectual capital simply as the value of the staff and human capital (classified as "employee competence" by Karl-Erik Sveiby) in the company. But there's much more to it than that. Larry Prusak, director of the IBM and Lotus initiative, defines IC as intellectual resources that have been "formalized, captured and leveraged" to create assets of higher value.[8] Thomas Stewart suggests the equally pithy "packaged useful knowledge."

In their work, Philip Bealieu, S. Mitchell Williams and Michael Wright from the University of Calgary define intellectual capital as: "The enhanced value of a firm attributable to assets, generally of an intangible nature, resulting from the company's organizational function, processes and information technology networks, the competency and efficiency of its employees and its relationship with its customers. Intellectual capital assets are developed from (a) the creation of new knowledge and innovation; (b) application of present knowledge to present issues and concerns that enhance employees and customers; (c) packaging, processing and transmission of knowledge; and (d) the acquisition of present knowledge created through research and learning."[9]

Structural capital is what remains within the company when people go home at night.

To my mind, intellectual capital is a combination of human capital – the brains, skills, insights and potential of those in an organization – and structural capital – things like the capital wrapped up in customers, processes, databases, brands and IT systems. It is the ability to transform knowledge and intangible assets into wealth creating resources, by multiplying human capital with structural capital.

The challenge (and it is not a new challenge, by the way) is to convert human capital – what employees know – into structural capital. Structural capital is what remains within the company when people go home at night. It is the knowledge recipes, which can be leveraged by someone else to the organization's benefit.

A simple analogy illustrates the point. Think of your computer. The financial value of the hardware decreases rapidly from the time you take it out of the box, but the value of its content increases exponentially. It grows every time you use it. What is the value that resides in the morass of semi-conductors and cables? It is your own intellectual capital captured as structural capital in the guts of the PC. The computer is tangible – you can touch it. Intellectual capital is ethereal – you cannot lay a finger on it. But together they create something greater than the sum of the parts – something which has a value.

Now, think of the physical embodiment of an organization. A company's structural capital lies in its work processes, knowledge recipes, filing cabinets, office design and so on. Its human capital is the knowledge and brains of the people who work for the organization – within and without its physical confines. The companies that succeed in future will be those that manage to entwine the two, so that structural capital remains even when the people leave the enterprise.

The third misunderstanding is to assume that intellectual capital is just another management fad. "I've generally thought of a business fad as being driven mainly by the attempt to sell something. So I did not use to think that label would apply to intellectual capital because there was nothing in particular to sell. Now with all this 'intranet' stuff, maybe that's not so true," said Tom Stewart when asked if intellectual capital was just another in a long line of management fads. "But still, intellectual capital or knowledge management, whatever we call it, is still a nascent field, hardly a juggernaut yet. And anyway, there is something to be said for fads. TQM may have become a fad, but quality still is a valuable concern. Re-engineering may have gotten bloated and used as an excuse for downsizing. But many of re-engineering's core ideas about value, focus, people, and innovation are important."[10]

Tony Buzan admits that he is worried that intellectual capital could become regarded as a fad. "Companies follow the fad because it's the route to competitive advantage. But they don't go deeper to what originated the fad in the first place," he says. "Whatever the fad what is the first thing companies have to teach their people? The first thing is to be able to learn and to be able to remember what they have learned. They have to learn to think and create and then apply it all to make some money. The trouble is that they don't do any of it.

"To lose £800,000 in a day, invest £1 million in training – 80 percent of what people learn is forgotten within a day of training. That isn't because training is inappropriate, it is because the training doesn't take into account the brain. Until training takes the brain into account, they'll continue to have new fads and new titular directors of the fads. They will continue to be disillusioned and search for the perfect fad, the panacea."[11]

Buzan goes on to provide a reminder of the business case for intellectual capital: "In the mid-1970s I gave a presentation to a group of senior executives. One of them said that it was really fascinating but what has the brain got to do with business? I recommended he went into his business and extracted the brains to have his answer.

"Imagine a company which is just the same as your own, a clone which opens up across the road. Each of the individuals in the newly cloned company is 10 percent more intelligent; 10 percent more relative; more fit; 10 percent faster in everything they do which requires speed; 10 percent healthier; 10 percent less stressed; 10 percent better at learning and thinking; 10 percent more energetic; 10 percent happier. How long would it take for the clone to dominate? What would happen to the other company? It wouldn't last long. The thing is that it is quite easy to become the alternative company."

Intellectual capital really is fundamental to all companies, communities and, even, societies.

Putting the issue of fads to one side, the fact remains that most value added in most businesses today is in the form of knowledge and intangibles, not materials. Some people appear to think that intellectual capital, Skandia and myself are indivisible, a holy trinity. But the entire point of intellectual capital is that it is universal. It doesn't just matter to one company. Intellectual capital really is fundamental to all companies, communities and, even, societies. It is not a management technique like re-engineering which you can choose to apply or not as the case may be. It is more fundamental than that.

Indeed, companies worldwide are leading the exploration of intellectual capital. Among them is the Canadian bank CIBC. "When the whole agenda is dominated by the financial results of the firm, it is difficult to understand how you can invest in [human development] and know that when you are investing in such intangible things that you're actually getting a tangible outcome," said Hubert Saint-Onge, when vice-president of learning organization and leadership development at CIBC.

Saint-Onge was then instrumental in the creation of a 60 person "knowledge-based lending group" exploring different means of defining credit worthiness rather than simply adding up tangible assets and holdings. To Saint-Onge learning and intellectual capital are inextricably linked. "What we find is that intellectual capital is the output of accelerated learning at the organizational level," he says. "Intellectual capital helps us determine or identify what the impact of our work is." Saint-Onge has now moved on to the very interesting position of senior vice-president of strategic capabilities at the Canadian life insurance group Clarica where he is instrumental in combining organizational innovations around IT and human capital as

> **Intellectual capital is the output of accelerated learning at the organizational level.**

well as measuring highly tacit dimensions of knowledge (such as the ability of values to create value). "We need to measure intellectual capital assets and concentrate more on the developmental factors that keep the organization healthy, vibrant and strong in its marketplace," he says.[12]

Or listen to the views of Lars Kolind, former CEO of the Danish company Oticon: "Intellectual capital, which in one way or the other is the difference between the stock value and the equity capital, increased from DKK 40–50 million to DKK 1.2 billion in four years. This is the difference between the value of a traditional company and a knowledge-based company. Information technology, boldness, management, ability to involve employees as partners are all-important elements. These are the sources of value."[13]

In fact, intellectual capital's pedigree is a lengthy one. Peter Drucker was talking about "knowledge workers" in the 1960s – in his classic *The Age of Discontinuity*. Recent years have seen a profusion of great minds being brought to bear on the subject – people like the true knowledge pioneer Karl-Erik Sveiby, *Fortune*'s Tom Stewart, Debra Amidon, Meg Wheatley, Larry Prusak, Paul Romer, and many, many more.

Its lengthy pedigree and intellectual credentials do not prevent people from interpreting intellectual capital very narrowly. Typically, companies appoint someone as chief knowledge officer or some such title and think that they understand intellectual capital fully and can develop management control over it.

Companies pay lip service to the concept because it is not easy. They prefer the quick fixes even when they realize that they do not work. Intellectual capital is not easy. It is not a corporate band-aid.

Even when knowledge can be codified, there is no guarantee that useful knowledge will be identified and exploited. A recent example involving British Telecommunications (BT) highlights the difficulties of practicing intellectual capital management. It has recently come to light that since the mid-1980s BT has been sitting on a US patent covering hyperlinks, one of the key building blocks of the world wide web.

The patent, which is potentially worth millions, if not billions, of dollars, remained buried in a filing cabinet in the company's vaults along with thousands of other global patents. At one level, the find underlines the importance of managing knowledge. At another, it illustrates that companies are not good at managing their intellectual properties. BT now faces an uphill legal battle to defend the patent.

Yet, despite such experiences and the elusive challenges it poses, intellectual capital is a concept whose time has come. This is the case because the nature of the business world and of the way we perceive the business world has changed. The new world is one in which the "dry science" of economics has been reincarnated and reinvigorated as knowledge economics.

COMPASS LINKS

www.skandia.se
www.clarica.com
www.sveiby.com.au
www.knowinc.com
www.entovation.com
www.intellectualcapital.se
www.baruch-lev.com

TAKING BEARINGS

- Who in your organization is responsible for intellectual capital?
- How does your organization value intellectual capital?
- How do you know the efficiency, rate of renewal and level of risk of your intellectual capital?
- How do you shape the learning department of the future?

HOW WE GOT HERE

1987   Karl-Erik Sveiby: *The Know-How Company*

Debra Amidon: *Managing the Knowledge Asset into the Twenty-First Century*

Thomas Johnson & Robert Kaplan: *Relevance Lost: The Rise and Fall of Management Accounting*

1989   Charles Handy: *The Age of Paradox*

Karl-Erik Sveiby: *The Invisible Balance Sheet*

1990   Peter Drucker: The New Realities in Government and Politics/in *Economics and Business*/in *Society and World View*

Charles Savage: *Fifth Generation Management*, *Dynamic Teaming*, *Virtual Enterprising* and *Knowledge Networking*

Peter Senge: *The Fifth Discipline*

1991   Leif Edvinsson appointed by Skandia as the world's first director of Intellectual Capital

James Brian Quinn: *Intelligent Enterprise*

Debra Amidon: *The Origins of a Knowledge-Based Firm*

Taichi Sakaiya: *Knowledge Value Revolution*

Ikujiro Nonaka: "Knowledge creating company" in *Harvard Business Review*

Tom Stewart: "Brainpower" in *Fortune*

1992   Jessica Lipnack: *The Age of the Network*

Meg Wheatley: *Leadership and the New Science*

Robert Kaplan and David Norton launch their concept of the Balanced Scorecard with an article in the *Harvard Business Review*

1993   Skandia and Leif Edvinsson prototype the first internal report on IC

1994   A Tom Stewart article on IC is the *Fortune* cover story

Mill Valley Group on IC networking meet for the first time

Hubert St Onge prototypes the concept of IC and customer capital

1995   Skandia presents the first public report on IC

1996   Skandia establishes its Future Center as an IC lab with Leif Edvinsson as Knowledge Leader

Baruch Lev establishes Intangibles Research at New York University

First IC of Nations report published by Caroline Stenfelt et al.

1997   IC hits the publishing trail with books by Leif Edvinsson & Michael Malone, Tom Stewart, Karl-Erik Sveiby (*The New Organizational Wealth*), Anne Brooking, as well as Göran Roos et al.

BBC produces a video on IC entitled "The new wealth of nations"

Nick Bontis presents the world's first PhD dissertation on IC

ICM gathering for Intellectual Property Rights launched in California by Pat Sullivan, Leif Edvinsson, and Gordon Petrash

1998   Nick Bontis and McMaster University in Canada organize the first large academic IC conference

Baruch Lev organizes the first IC accounting conference

SEC initiates research on intangible assets at Brookings Institute, Washington

IC Rating launched by Intellectual Capital Sweden

Brain Trust Foundation awards Leif Edvinsson the Brain of the Year prize for his pioneering work on IC

1999   EU begins a measurement project on IC: Meritum and NIMCube

Future Centre ABB inaugurated

2000   Establishment of Knowledge Management Forum, Henley Management College, UK

Sydkraft Future Center inaugurated

The Journal of IC launched

Government of Denmark publishes first guidelines for IC accounting

Skandia initiates IC Vision and IC Community

2001   Lund establishes the first professorship on IC and appoints Leif Edvinsson as the first holder of the position

The EU's High Level Group publishes its first major report on intangibles

Jan Mouritsen et al. of Copenhagen Business School publish "IC and the capable firm"

Brookings Institute publishes its report *Unseen Wealth*

Future Center Norway inaugurated

Baruch Lev's *Intangibles Management*, *Measurement & Reporting* published

SEC and FASB in USA publicly advocates IC reporting

OECD publish *Score Board 2001 – Towards a Knowledge Based Economy*

Notes

1   Ingrid Tidhult has written a diary of the first years of the Skandia Future Center, entitled *Memories from the Future*

2   Dilani, Alan, "Design & health – therapeutic benefits of design," Karolinska Institute, Stockholm 2001

3   Interview with Tony Buzan

4   Strassmann, Paul, "Calculating knowledge capital," *Knowledge Management*, October 1999

5   This was published in *Fortune* in 2001 as "The smartest companies in the USA".

6   Interview

7   Knowledge management includes managing information (explicit/recorded knowledge); managing processes (embedded knowledge); managing people (tacit knowl-edge); managing innovation (knowledge conversion); and managing assets (intellectual capital).

8   Manasco, Britton, "Leading companies focus on managing and measuring intellectual capital," *Knowledge Inc.*, undated

9   Beaulieu, Philip; Williams, S Mitchell; & Wright, Michael, *Intellectual capital disclosure practices in Scandinavia*

10 Perelman, Lewis, "Tom Stewart on knowledge," *Knowledge Inc.*, 1997

11 Interview

12 Manasco, Britton, "Leading companies focus on managing and measuring intellectual capital," *Knowledge Inc.*, undated

13 Danish Trade and Industry Development Council, 1996

The New Knowledge Economics

The economics of goods and markets have given way to the economics of knowledge and the migration of knowledge.

SO LONG ADAM SMITH?

How can I be so sure that intellectual capital is important and will become increasingly so in the years to come? Simply, we now live in the intangible economy. Knowledge economics is the new reality. Minds matter.

The most enthusiastic champions of the new economy have claimed that knowledge economics marks the demise of conventional economic wisdom. This is over-stating the new economy's revolutionary powers. Even so, traditional economics is being questioned.

The Santa Fe Institute's W. Brian Arthur is among the most coherent commentators on this subject. Arthur's central gripe about economics as a discipline is that it has become distanced from reality. "I would like to see economics become more of a science, and more of a science means that it concerns itself more with reality," he says. "We're facing a danger that economics is rigorous deduction based upon faulty assumptions."[1] It is not that economics is wrong, but that our assumptions are wrong.

In a technically and intellectually based economy, the rules of economics are being challenged and changed. Understanding of the new commercial realities requires radical new insights from radical new economists.

Most notably, the law of diminishing returns has been turned on its head to produce the law of increasing returns. This means that under certain circumstances companies can quickly come to totally dominate a market. Such is the power of increasing returns that the power of market forces appears negated – indeed, for a while it is. The invisible hand of market forces is "a little bit arthritic," notes Arthur.

"The physical world is characterized by diminishing returns," observes Stanford's Paul Romer. "Diminishing returns are a result of the scarcity of physical objects. One of the most important differences between objects and ideas ... is that ideas are not scarce and the process of discovery in the realm of ideas does not suffer from diminishing returns."[2] We are dealing with the economics of the exponential potential of knowledge recipes.

Underpinning these arguments is a move away from solutions and foolproof models to questions, frameworks and knowledge recipes. Says Brian Arthur: "Economics has always taken a shortcut and said, assume there is a problem and assume that we can arrive at a solution. Now, I would say, assume there's a situation, how do players cognitively deal with it? In other words, what frameworks do they wheel up to understand the situation." Making sense of the situation is the critical first step. Assuming there is an economic model, which will spit out a solution, is a sure route to diminishing returns.

Of course, new insights do not constitute new economics. In fact, many of the basics remain unchanged. The fundamentals of demand and supply have not altered; nor for that matter has the imperative for businesses to make money. What can be said is that economics now has to be understood in a different perspective, a longitudinal and lateral perspective.

You can put things in context by looking back to the early days of the factory, the railroad, the automobile, and especially the harnessing of electricity. If you do so, a lot of what seems new about the Internet starts to look familiar. The true commercial revolution took place in Western Europe some 500 or so years ago. A

> **One of the most important differences between objects and ideas ... is that ideas are not scarce.**

complete break with the past, it paved the way for subsequent technology-led revolutions. It was built on one of the key realizations of the age. Summed up by the economist Adam Smith in his book *The Wealth of Nations* (1776), it asserted that the true wealth of a nation is measured not by how much gold it possesses, but by what it can produce.

Smith argued that the value of a particular good or service is determined by the costs of production. If something is expensive to produce, then its value is similarly high. "What is bought with money or with goods is purchased by labour, as much as what we acquire by the toil of our own body ... They contain the value of a certain quantity of labour which we exchange for what is supposed at the time to contain the value of an equal quantity," wrote Smith in *The Wealth of Nations*.

Smith crowned productivity and it has reigned supreme ever since. This laid the foundation for a series of technology-related revolutions – of which the Internet is the most recent.

Productivity was best achieved and improved through the advancement of technology and the division of labor. "The division of labour ... occasions in every art, a proportional increase of the productive powers of labour," Smith wrote. "The separation of different trades and employments from one another seems to have taken place in consequence of this advantage."

This system of maximizing productivity through technology and demarcation provided the basis for the management theorists of the early twentieth century, such as scientific management champion, Frederick Taylor, and practitioners such as Henry Ford. They translated the economic rigor of Smith's thinking to practices in the workplace. They did so in ways and to a scale, which Smith could never have imagined.

> **Productivity was best achieved and improved through the advancement of technology and the division of labor.**

If productivity was the goal, efficient processes were the means of achieving the goal. According to Charles Lucier and Janet Torsilieri of management consulting firm Booz-Allen & Hamilton, a process-driven model of management has dominated our minds ever since Adam Smith.[3] We have been engaged in maximizing the efficiency of our processes whether we are widget-makers or McDonald's. Efficient, lean processes with cost-efficient overheads have become regarded as the quickest route to profit heaven.

Companies continue to pursue efficiency through lean and, therefore, they hope, productive, organizational structures. The quest for leanness is often a tortured one, as any dieter will tell you. Indeed, leanness pretty soon leads to the corporate equivalent of anorexia, organizations emptied of people, experience, values, meaning and value in all its manifestations. Leanness depersonalizes.

Leanness has proved difficult to achieve anyway. Good intentions have not been matched by reality. "Overhead in major corporations is not decreasing," note the consultants Lucier and Torsilieri. One contributory factor to this is the rise of professional experts. This relies on the division of mental labor rather than an over-riding emphasis on creating processes to divide physical labor.

As Lucier and Torsilieri's work suggests, we are engaged in a re-evaluation of Adam Smith and traditional economics rather than a complete rewriting. Productivity still matters. It is just that our understanding of productivity and how to achieve it has changed and will change. "Adam Smith realized that the factory model would 'stupify' people. The Knowledge Era creates opportunities that 'smartify' people in exciting and unexpected ways," says Charles Savage of Knowledge Era Enterprises.[4]

Clearly, history puts its own limitations on Adam Smith's theorizing. Physical labor is no longer so important. The twentieth century saw the emergence of management as a profession – it is barely acknowledged by Smith. Similarly, Smith wrote without knowledge of the power and scope of modern corporations – let alone the power of brand names and customer loyalty. He also wrote in harder times where self-interest was not a choice but a necessity.

What is changing is the way we understand what is being supplied and what is traded. Labor may be mental, but is still divided and has to migrate. This in turn changes the way we price goods and services; and changes the entire notion of value and the dynamics of value.

At the heart of knowledge economics is the entire notion of intangible value, the role of intangible assets in value creation and the exponential multiplier effect of knowledge recipes. In the knowledge economy, what has a value today may be different to what had a value yesterday, and tomorrow.

The fact is that the nature of competitive advantage has shifted from the physical to the intangible; the visible to the invisible; the seen to the unseen. The nature of value creation is going through a paradigm change. The question is what sort of paradigm change?

In their book *Information Rules*, Carl Shapiro and Hal Varian lay out some of the lessons economics offers for business strategy. Of central importance is the changing nature of competitive advantage – not based on market position, size and power as in times past, but on the incorporation of knowledge into all of an organization's activities. Knowledge-based competitive advantages include the power of intangible assets as signals of value; standards like Microsoft's operating systems or the English language; innovations protected through patents, copyrights or secrecy, as with Merck or Coca-Cola; or simply a reputation for innovation as Sony enjoys.

Adam Smith could not have imagined the growing importance of services. In Sweden only 22 percent of people employed in industry can now be categorized as blue-collar workers. Of these, perhaps half could be categorized as knowledge workers of some sort – they are qualified engineers or supervisors. In a high-tech modern factory, a cutting machine supervisor is essentially a knowledge worker.

In the United States, services have increased steadily as a share of measured total output in the economy, from 22 percent of GDP in 1950 to about 39 percent of GDP in 1999.[5] Intangibles such as skills or professional knowledge, organizational capabilities, reputational capital, mailing lists or other collections of data, tend to be important factors in the provision of many services. In the United States investment in intangibles passed that of tangibles in 1992. Little wonder that intangibles are now driving the economy. In October 2001 OECD published *Score Board 2001 – Towards a Knowledge Based Economy*.

Smith had little time for services. Eighteenth-century Britain was even less of a service economy than twenty-first-century Britain. Writing over two hundred years ago, Smith held that only material goods add to the stock of a nation's capital, and characterized services as "vanishing in the instant they are performed." Others held the view that services really were productive, as has been recognized intuitively by many companies for a long time. But the processes involved are complex and have not yielded readily to analytical methods. As a result their productivity and value-added mechanisms are notoriously difficult to measure. Over the past decade there have been a number of attempts to devise a new taxonomy for the economy that is theoretically meaningful and useful for empirical analysis, but these have been severely constrained by a lack of broadly accepted definitions.

In the knowledge economy, the relationship between labor invested and price is looser. Knowledge workers are expensive, but their output can be sold and re-sold many times – although their shelf life may be much more limited. (Knowledge is perishable and quickly becomes obsolete.) The value of many goods and services is now based on the intellect embedded in them.

In the knowledge economy value is becoming experiential. There is something, which is even worse than a service for completing a vanishing act: an idea. "We have taken the fixed quantity of matter available to us and rearranged it. We have changed things from a form that is less valuable into a form that is more valuable. Value creation and wealth creation in their most basic senses have to do with taking physical objects and rearranging them," explains Stanford's Paul Romer, who distinguishes between human capital and ideas. "Ideas are the recipes we use to rearrange things to create more value and wealth. For example, we have ideas about ways to make steel by combining iron with carbon and a few other elements. We have ideas about how to take silicon – an abundant element that was almost worthless to us until recently – and make it into semiconductor chips. So, we have physical materials to work with – raw ingredients – which are finite and scarce and we have ideas or knowledge, which tell us how to use those raw materials ... There are always more recipes that we can find to combine raw materials in ways that make them more valuable to us."[6]

Ideas and rapid learning are the new currency. The invisible hand of economics discussed by Adam Smith just became a lot more elusive. The hard science of economics has become softer around the edges – indeed, the Japanese have been referring to "softnomics" for a number of years.

useful way to explain

COMPASS LINKS
www.santafe.edu
www.stanford.edu
www.strassman.com
www.kee-inc.com
www.oecd.org/publications
www.dieverwandlungderwelt.de

TAKING BEARINGS
- What are your main intangible competitive advantages?
- How much of the work in your organization is codified into knowledge recipes?
- How much of your annual expenses go into intangibles compared to tangibles?

THE BATTLE FOR THOUGHT LEADERSHIP

Ideas are, perhaps, the most ethereal resources at an organization's disposal. They fall through the cracks of intellectual property law with worrying ease. They defy classification. No one knows this better than those who work in the great ideas sectors of our age: business schools and consulting firms. Where better to look for clues of where the knowledge economy is headed?

In May 2000 the great and the good of the business school world gathered in bucolic Hanover, New Hampshire. No doubt with a plentiful supply of canapés and martinis, they were there to celebrate the 100th anniversary of the founding of Dartmouth College's Tuck School of Business. There were many reasons to be cheerful. But, beneath the jolly exterior trouble loomed.

Included in the events, was a one-day symposium to look at intellectual property rights. Richard L. Schmalensee, dean of MIT Sloan School of Management, warned that a looming dispute between b-schools and their faculty over intellectual property rights (IPR) could be "a major earthquake zone."

The big talking point at this gathering was who benefits – the schools or their faculty – from the increasing provision of web-based management education courses. On-line management education courses are big business. Providers of web-based business education such as the University of Phoenix in the US, IBM, which has partnered with Wharton, and UNext, which has contracted courses from Columbia, Stanford, Carnegie-Mellon, the University of Chicago and the London School of Economics, are just the tip of an explosion of web-based distance learning management education. Recently MIT put most of its learning material on the web. But who owns the rights to the course materials for these on-line upstarts? As you might have guessed, the answer appears to be b-school faculty. Effectively, b-school faculty work for the competition. And the competition pays more!

> **Intellectual property rights (IPR) could be "a major earthquake zone."**

Although no-one is saying exactly how much faculty earn from writing on-line courses, it is rumoured to be significant, perhaps in the hundreds of thousands of dollars range. Certainly, it's a lot more than most academics earn from writing books, to which the schools generally turn a blind eye, allowing the writers to keep all royalties. Indeed, many academics write books on sabbaticals, leaving the schools uninvolved.

Robert Sullivan, dean of Kenan-Flagler business school in North Carolina, accepted that faculty could be involved with competing with their own institutions but was equally concerned with how schools can reward faculty for giving up their intellectual property. "Faculty who write text books normally get all the royalties. The book model has never been challenged," agreed Sullivan. "But who owns intellectual capital that is digitally captured? There are real issues about using interactive teaching tools to replace faculty. People are concerned about that. We are asking them to give up something of real value to them. And then schools get involved with outside, commercial companies that 'package' this material, they also have rights. It's a very complex issue."

> **Understanding who owns ideas is critical to the future of business.**

Another question concerns who really owns this intellectual property. Perhaps it isn't the business schools after all. As Dean Sullivan points out, most faculty have developed their ideas over many years spent at a number of academic institutions. But perhaps it isn't individual faculty either. Faculty members who teach on particular courses each bring something of themselves to the course. Faculty share cases, notes, exams and so on. The course is enhanced and developed year after year. A prestigious General Management Program at a big b-school is not solely the creation of the faculty you see before you, but probably a generation of faculty. Structural capital is embedded in the courses themselves.

Academics are not renowned for their willingness to get on amiably with one another. But the entire IPR issue is more than a storm in a genteel teacup. It is further proof that ideas are the true currency of the world. B-school professors trade in ideas. Understanding where ideas originate and how they are disseminated, and who owns them or benefits from them, is critical to the future of business schools. Who owns ideas is a matter of frenzied debate in Silicon Valley, in the software hotbed of Bangalore, in the

UK's Silicon Fen, in industry after industry. The debate defies geography. Whose ideas are they anyway is the new refrain. It is also the key to the future of all organizations.

This also explains the tremendous rise of corporate universities. These internal sources of executive development have emerged from the fringes to become major players in executive development. They challenge business schools and also make a clear statement: developing people is a crucial business issue.

Not too far from the business schools – geographically or intellectually – another battle is being fought out daily. A peek into the mysterious world of the management consulting industry reveals another side to the ideas coin.

Organizations might be regarded as collections of ideas. This has long been appreciated in the management consulting. Here, ideas are the lifeblood. In such businesses, it is a competitive advantage to have more and better ideas. In consulting-speak, the war of ideas is the quest for "thought leadership." The company, which leads in thought processing, leads in the market place.

Yet even this is not so straightforward. The firm that clients believe to lead a particular field enjoys a competitive advantage. Much rests on the credibility of the firm and its ability to convey to the market that it has the best solutions.

The traditional leader in this field is McKinsey & Company. McKinsey does not advertise. McKinsey bolsters its brand through the *McKinsey Quarterly*, a serious, heavyweight publication which has been around for 35 years and which sometimes makes the *Harvard Business Review* appear frivolous by comparison.

Most of the big strategy-based consulting firms are involved in the thought leadership battle. "Thought leadership is the only place for the top firms. They can't compete on price or on results. But only two firms – McKinsey and the Boston Consulting Group (BCG) – have done it consistently," says Sam Hill who led Booz-Allen & Hamilton's move into the thought leadership melée. "It is a great strategy. Ideas are the single best source of differentiation. They also mean that you can use PR instead of advertising, which is much more credible. The trouble is that it is not easy to do."[7] In many ways, Booz-Allen's strategy reaped more benefits than most. Prior to taking the thought leadership route, it was largely unheralded, a lesser light next to the intellectual beacons of McKinsey, Bain and BCG. Now, Booz-Allen is actively involved in the intellectual battle. Its consulting stars are quoted and referred to. Column inches are the payback. (Perhaps they could be labeled "the return on shared thought.")

Why do I tell you all this? Well, simply, consulting firms compete on the basis of thought leadership. Sometimes these are codified into intellectual property. Mostly they are intangible knowledge recipes. The difference between McKinsey and Bain is not about how much they charge (a lot) or the way they work (much the same), but in the intellectual vigor and originality they bring to each problem they face. That represents value to clients. Of course, vigor and originality reside largely in the mind of the beholder. In the knowledge economy, thought leadership is a source of competitive advantage. It represents a kind of generic temporary information monopoly.

COMPASS LINKS
www.bah.com
www.consultinginfo.com
www.mbaplanet.com
www.corpu.com
www.mit.edu

TAKING BEARINGS
- Who are the thought leaders in your enterprise sector?
- How do you track thought processing?
- How are you ensuring that you become a thought leader – personally and organizationally?
- What are the most tangible parts of your thought processing?
- How do you communicate thought processes?
- Who owns your ideas?
- Who owns your company's ideas?
- Who owns your competitor's ideas?
- Who is copying your ideas?

THOUGHT MODELS

Ideas and what we do with them – thought processing – matters. Knowledge intensive firms fight over the latest ideas because they know that innovations are the route to sustainable attractiveness.

Apply this at an organizational level and we see that companies compete on the strength of their "thought models." The models by which they generate ideas, manage ideas, capitalize on ideas and maximize the commercial potential of ideas are the source of advantage. A company's ability to generate new business thought models is strategically critical.

Adrian Slywotzky has noted that the last business revolution was led by innovative companies, which changed the question they asked themselves. The question that enlightened strategists asked in the 1980s was "What business are you in?" (Answers, as always, were thin on the ground or better left on the ground.) In the early 1990s, the key question changed as a new generation looked at what companies such as Dell were doing and began asking, "What is your business model?"[8] Now it might be time to ask: What is your thought model? How do you process innovative thinking?

There is a great deal of talk of business models. As I write, Xerox has announced that it is struggling once again. Its problem? Wrong model. Business models are better described as thought models, ways of thinking about a particular business or a particular way of doing business.

Look at the example of Priceline. In many ways, the company was the original dot-com. In 1998, its $15 million radio advertising blitz captured the American public's imagination. The ads invited consumers to log on and name their price for airline tickets. Disbelief rapidly turned to wonder, as Priceline became a household name. Few appreciated that Jay Walker, the man behind Priceline, was using the Internet to leverage the previously hidden economics of airline yield management. Few cared. In its first year, the company generated revenues of $35 million. Its IPO in March 1999, valued the company at $13 billion. (As I write, it has plummeted to a fraction of this valuation.)

The important thing about Priceline is that Jay Walker has made a business out of patenting different ways of doing business, new business thought models, and then leveraging them.

Walker discovered that it was possible to patent a thought model providing it satisfies the basic tests of patentability. It must be unique and non-obvious. Once patented, in theory, the originator owns the business recipe, providing he or she has the money to enforce it in law. Through his company Walker Digital, Jay Walker has filed for over 200 patents, including the "name-your-price" concept. (Similarly, Amazon.com sought to patent its one-click methodology for making purchases.)

While Walker's use of patents was innovative, patents and the protection of ideas is hardly a new thing. Indeed, intellectual protection was a right given to a person in the ancient Sybarite society. (Though the right usually only lasted for a year.) A little later, Article 1, Section 8, Clause 8 of the American Constitution gave Congress the power "to promote the Progress of Science and useful Arts, by securing for limited Times to Authors and Inventors the exclusive Right to their respective Writings and Discoveries." In 1790, Congress acted on this authority and enacted the first patent act. Thomas Jefferson was the country's first "patent examiner."

Regardless of the final outcome of the Priceline story, Jay Walker has demonstrated that entire businesses may be built around a thought model rather than a range of products or carefully delineated services.

A business thought model is an idea in search of an organization to make it work and create value. The next challenge is the shortening life expectancy among these recipes for enterprise success. Companies must create new ways of thinking and then do so again. They must constantly renew. The issue then is the efficiency and effectiveness of their thought processes, their ability to think, capture thinking and to convert it into financial value; intellectual capital.[9] Another way to express this challenge is how you realize value from the IC assets of your enterprise?

COMPASS LINKS
www.icmgroup.com
www.priceline.com

TAKING BEARINGS
- Which enterprise in your sector would be most likely to come up with a new value creating thought model?
- What are the key characteristics of your thought-processing model?
- How can the Internet change your value creating thought model?
- How much time do you spend considering alternative thought models?

FORGET PRODUCTS;
THINK KNOWLEDGE RECIPES

B-schools, consulting firms and thought model originators like Priceline share a single lesson. We now compete in terms of intangibles and thought processing. In the past this was not the case – or, at least, was not thought to be the case. The received wisdom was that companies sought to be different through producing different products. This was the world of Adam Smith where labor was rigorously divided to produce the most products in the least possible time. Companies invested time and energy in coming up with new products, slightly different products, enhanced versions of old products. They tinkered and changed with dedication. Some continue to do so.

We now compete in terms of intangibles and thought processing.

The trouble for them is that the knowledge economy requires new perspectives. It is useful, therefore, to think of products and things in a new light, an entirely new light. We tend to think of perishable commodities as products like fruit, vegetables, and fish. But today, knowledge is a perishable commodity. Companies that do not refresh their knowledge store end up with the equivalent of rotting fish in their warehouses. The arrival of refrigeration meant that people started freezing perishable commodities like fish. (Eventually, of course, they still have to be thawed to be used, but we'll come to that.) The same now applies to other products and services. In the knowledge economy, companies could regard their offerings as frozen knowledge or codified knowledge to be shared rapidly on a global and local basis.

Some products are easier to imagine like this than others. Take maps. Looking at antique maps, it is obvious that they represent the limits of the cartographer's knowledge at the time. Early maps showed a world that most people thought was flat. Over the centuries, whole new continents were added as explorers uncovered vast new lands and added to the cartographers' knowledge. Maps changed in other ways, too. A Victorian map would show the British Empire, a large part of the world, in pink. Today, the pink has gone. That world is history-frozen.

In the Skandia Future Center there is a wonderful antique globe. On its surface is the night sky, the constellations reconfigured to fit around the surface of a papier maché globe. It is a thing of beauty. But in essence, a globe is frozen knowledge. With this globe the knowledge is made tangible through the imagination of its creator. The artist reconfigured the stars in the sky into the shape of a globe. Knowledge is transformed via the human imagination into a thing, which potentially lives long after its creator.

An interesting question, which arises from this historical example, is how we understand cyberspace. Is cyberspace a globe? Certainly it offers a global window on what companies are doing. On the Internet we confront the globalization of knowledge. At the click of a mouse, it is possible to garner information about what a company is doing on the other side of the world. It is possible to copy its products. But it is much harder to duplicate its knowledge.

The point is an important one. If we think of products in terms of knowledge they are robust competitive weapons. Your competitors can copy your product tomorrow. They are **To achieve sustainable earnings you have to create knowledge recipes.** probably hard at work copying and improving on it as you read this. And, much worse, someone, somewhere, can also make your product more cheaply and more efficiently.

So, what do you bring to the party? Well, if you are to achieve sustainable earnings you have to create knowledge recipes, which freeze your organization's knowledge in a moment in time. Your knowledge must be at the leading edge. It must be uniquely yours. And it must embody the collective knowledge of the entire organization rather than a small part of it. And it has to be migrated rapidly around the globe.

Then comes the twist in the tale, like light from a distant star. By the time we hold the product in our hands the knowledge that created it has already moved on. We know, for example, that by the time we install the very latest software release on our computers, the next version is already well advanced in some lab in Silicon Valley or Redmond, Washington. This leads to the quest for fast companies and embedded knowledge.

In the knowledge economy, this applies to all companies. In the time it takes the competition to replicate that product, your company will need new knowledge to freeze. Fast companies require fast, innovative knowledge to be cloned and capitalized. This is what David Skyrme calls the move from e-business to k-business.[10]

COMPASS LINKS
www.fastcompany.com
www.skyrme.com
www.kwork.org

TAKING BEARINGS
- In what way are your products frozen knowledge?
- How do you embed knowledge recipes in the value proposals you offer to customers?
- How do you codify your knowledge recipes?
- How do you clone your knowledge recipes as well mutate them into new knowledge innovations?

THE INTANGIBLE HAND

Ideas are the new currency. You can't touch them. Ideas are intangible. But just because we can't see or touch something, doesn't mean it doesn't exist. It is there.

Intangibles are the driving force of the new knowledge economics. We have moved from an economy driven by tangibles – products, things – to one driven by intangibles – ideas, concepts, abstracts.

Think of it; for some companies, like America Online and Microsoft, around 90 percent of their market capitalization value lies in intangibles. Microsoft has very little in the way of physical plant and equipment. Indeed, at one time, Microsoft had only $1.6 billion in property, plant and equipment, but a market capitalization heading towards $400 billion. That's a lot of stuff people know little or nothing about and which people have not sought to quantify. The great corporation of our times is an illusion – albeit a lucrative one. "Given that no company can establish a monopoly on brains, how do you keep the people that make it work? There are no tangible assets to divest. There is intellectual property and that's about it – and a building," attorney Lloyd Cutler commented on the proposed breakup of Microsoft.[11]

Intangible assets can account for 90 percent of a company's value. According to Andrew Mayo, in his book *The Human Value of the Enterprise*, in late 2000 a total of 74 percent of BP's value was accounted for by intangible assets. For 3M the figure was 82 percent. Okay, 3M is in the ideas business, but how about an industrial conglomerate? Surely ABB would have lots of hard assets and fewer intangible ones? Not so, 85 percent of ABB's assets at that time were categorized as intangible.[12]

A number of individuals and organizations have been wrestling with the challenges and potential of intangibles. In 2000 the European Community launched a study of "policy trends in intangible assets" in seven member states and set up a European High Level Expert Group (HLEG) under the leadership of Clark Eustace to examine the subject. The HLEG took intangibles to be: "Non-material factors that contribute to enterprise performance in the production of goods or the provision of services, or that are expected to generate future economic benefits to the entities or individuals that control their deployment."[13] The Group went on to conclude: "Even when we can visualize them, their intrinsic characteristics make intangibles difficult to track. Because we cannot see them, touch them or weigh them, we cannot measure them directly and have to rely on proxy or indirect measures of their impact. In both macro and business economics, their existence is revealed indirectly by incremental economic performance that is not accounted for by the conventional key indicators."[14]

In his work Peter Hill refers to "immaterial goods" and suggests they make up a third class of economic activity (in addition to goods and services). Hill defines immaterial goods as non-physical entities that can be separated from a firm's organizational fabric – generally in the form of intellectual property (patents, licenses, trademarks, etc.) as distinct from those which are interwoven, often in complex and subtle ways, with the enterprise's physical and financial asset base. Such goods can be bought, sold, stocked, licensed and otherwise traded in the same manner as physical goods:

• They consist mainly, possibly exclusively, of immaterial
   products in the form of information and scientific, literary,
   artistic or entertainment creations that are generally recorded
   and stored on media such as paper, film, tape or disk.

- They have all the essential economic characteristics of goods – often highly durable goods – and, as such, have nothing in common with services, although physical goods and services may be deployed as carriers and distribution agencies, often in electronic form.
- They are generally sub-classes of IPR, which offers the advantage of an established framework of definitions that is recognized internationally.
- Under current accounting and SNA conventions, they are not reflected in the stock of material wealth until a transfer of ownership takes place.
- They represent the prime stocks of the intangible economy, and should be disclosed as such.

However they are defined, there is no doubt that the power of intangibles is growing. The Brookings Institution found that in 1962, 62 percent of a company's value was represented by its physical, or hard, capital.[15] By 1992 the percentage had declined to 38 percent. It is still falling. Other research cited by the University of Calgary's Mitchell Williams showed that on average in 1995 over 75 percent of the value of companies from the health care and personal services industries was attributed to the entity's intellectual capital.[16]

Stern University's Baruch Lev has carried out world leading research in this area. He found that in 1929 approximately 70 percent of American investments went into tangible goods and some 30 percent into intangibles. By 1990 this pattern was inverted, and today the dominant investment is in intangibles, such as R&D, education and competencies, IT software and the Internet. This applies to a large number of countries. On average, more than 10 percent of GDP in OECD countries is calculated to go into intangibles. For countries like Sweden this input is estimated to be more than 20 percent of GDP. Since 1992 in the United States, more than $200 billion has been invested in intangibles every year. Indeed, one estimate put American investment in intangibles in 2000 at a staggering $1000 billion.[17]

This is also reflected in stock prices. According to Lev, market value and book value were roughly equivalent in the late 1970s.

During the 1990s the average market-to-book ratio increased sharply and, according to the consulting firm McKinsey, is now greater than three, while for technology and software stocks (excluding the dot-coms, which break all the rules), it can go as high as 50 or more. (On average for the New York Stock exchange the figure is six.)

What you can't see is now driving the economies of the world. The intangible intellectual capital of nations is the new wealth of nations. Capital is not just financial; capital is something – any thing – which adds new wealth. Period.

Intangibility is the driving force behind the so-called new economy. In America, the Intellectual Property Association has estimated that the creative sectors – chiefly communications, information, entertainment, science and technology – are already worth $360 billion a year, making them more valuable than automobiles, aerospace or agriculture.

Indeed, while there is a lot of talk of the new economy, I'm not sure that it is the right adjective. After all, today's economy is always new. Things move on. Perhaps it is more useful to regard it as a new sphere for value creation, an intangible sphere or intellectual capital sphere. This requires genuinely new ways of looking at things, of expressing what we see and experience, and new ways of quantifying and measuring. That's where the newness lies. It is a new perspective, a longitude perspective, and the right description might be knowledge economics.

COMPASS LINKS
www.brookings.edu/es/researc h www.ll-a.fr/intangibles/ www.wissenskapital.info

TAKING BEARINGS
- What investment flows into tangibles and intangibles are evident in your country, region or company?
- Which intangible assets are key to the future of your enterprising?
- How do you measure and cultivate those assets?

MARKETS IN KNOWLEDGE

Take the concept of knowledge economics to its purest essence and you find yourself trading in knowledge. Forget the price of gold or of tin or cocoa beans. How about the price of your knowledge recipes? What's the going rate for your thought model?

Knowledge can be an expensive commodity. The share price of a company can go up or down on the strength of available knowledge. Take the case of the UK biotech company Antisoma. What happened to the company in mid-2000 demonstrates the power of knowledge. One minute, Antisoma was riding high on the potential of a new treatment it was developing for ovarian cancer. Then a Ph.D. student delivered a paper at a cancer conference several thousand miles away in the US, which cast doubt on its lead product, and wiped 40 percent off the company's market value. The paper, presented by Steven Nicholson, a Ph.D. student and doctor at St George's Hospital in London, prompted Antisoma to suspend clinical trials on its flagship product Theragyn to examine Nicholson's study. One man's knowledge can have a powerful impact in knowledge enterprising.

The incident underlines the volatility of biotech shares, but it also highlights a troublesome management issue. As information becomes ever more widely available, private individuals exert a growing influence over the fortunes of entire companies. This process is compounded by the Internet. Until recently, large organizations maintained power through the management of information inside and outside their borders. Today, that is no longer possible.

Managing knowledgeable outsiders may be one of the corporate insider's biggest jobs.

Companies are struggling to get to grips with the power shift that enables lone gunmen and women to dent their carefully constructed corporate image. They can be assailed from unlikely places. The Hollywood film industry, for example, now has to reckon with Harry Knowles, a lone film-buff who posts film reviews on his www.aint-it-cool-news.com site from his home in Austin, Texas. Similarly, Matt Drudge is a thorn in the side of the US political and journalistic establishment. Drudge sniped his way to fame when his Internet news site, the Drudge Report, broke the Monica

Lewinsky story – scooping the combined Washington press corps. In the years to come, managing knowledgeable outsiders may be one of the corporate insider's biggest jobs.

There has always been a market for knowledge. The publishing industry is based on it. But today the Internet is making the distribution of knowledge ever easier. The days when the publisher decided what got published are over. Today anyone with a PC and a modem can talk to the world. This is reducing the friction in the knowledge economy as well as transaction value. The Internet spawns new possibilities. We all have knowledge but until now we had no way to trade it except through our jobs. The enterprise was the arena for trading knowledge under the umbrella label of employment.

Think of the possibilities. Everyone has knowledge in whatever industry he or she is in. For example, say you are a computer dealer. Over the years you have compiled a list of the ten best lowest price places to buy wholesale computer equipment. You can sell your knowledge to newer, younger computer dealers who have no way to find this knowledge without losing thousands of dollars finding out the hard way. Why not?

The future lies in "knowledge exchange" as much as "knowledge sharing." The future lies in the use of markets within, as well as outside, organizations to facilitate intellectual capital development. "There is much value in [developing] market mechanisms which create more efficient markets for knowledge," contends Larry Prusak of the Institute of Knowledge Management. "These markets enable 'buyers and sellers' of knowledge to exchange their goods at a 'market-derived' price."[18] These will be the third generation of exchanges, auctions for thought recipes. The first exchanges were the raw material exchanges, which began life hundreds of years ago. Second came the financial exchanges, which arose some hundred years ago. And now we see the emergence of the third generation; knowledge exchanges.

Bryan Davis, a knowledge management expert, believes that knowledge markets and exchanges are a new trillion dollar market place in the making. "We are now witnessing the explosion and formation of a new galaxy, an economy fired by brainpower. This is about connections and contexts – expanding synapses in the Global

Brain," he says.[19] And it gets better. Knowledge is a renewable resource. Better yet, it actually increases with use. Paul Romer has sagely suggested that knowledge has the distinct advantage of being the only asset that grows with use. Knowledge does not wear itself out, it grows and grows as surely as a benevolent virus.

So what does this mean? Well, it opens up exciting new vistas. Take the website, www.knexa.com, which facilitates the exchange and trade of knowledge assets globally. (While Knexa.com focuses on B2B, IntraKnexa covers organizational knowledge sharing.) Based in Vancouver, British Columbia, Knexa is pioneering the concept of the knowledge exchange auction. It is one of the first exchanges in the world where users may buy and sell their knowledge and experience online. Knexa estimates

Knowledge is the only asset that grows with use.

that in 1998 the "Global Brain" created $5 trillion of intellectual capital. Of this, a mere 2 percent was traded or exchanged. That means that 98 percent remains under-exploited. The problem until now has been the lack of a marketplace for this sort of knowledge.[20]

Knexa.com's chief knowledge officer Nick Bontis explains: "Knexa.com represents a wonderful nexus of three pervasive phenomena: the ubiquitous access to information that the Internet offers; the sophisticated but user-friendly dynamics of auction-based technology; and, market-based valuation of intellectual capital."

Today, it may sound far-fetched, but there is plenty of evidence to suggest that the concept could work. Datamonitor, a global market analysis firm, projected in a recent study that Internet "information exchanges" will generate transaction revenues of $6bn annually by the year 2005, facilitating over $50bn of online purchases. The Datamonitor study also projected that knowledge management and exchange over the Internet will "create a new Internet sector with $30bn in market capitalizations." Already there are sites like *Fatbrain.com*, *Xpertsite.com*, *Exp.com*, and *ExpertCentral.com* where knowledge is the primary currency. There have also been early knowledge exchange prototypes including IQ-port from NatWest and KnowNet from PDVS/the University of Valencia, Venezuela.

Auctions make up over 20 percent of the top e-commerce sites on the Web. Forrester Research rated online auctions as one of the top three emerging B2B e-commerce models and also predicts this market will grow dramatically over the next few years. Vernon Keenan, an Internet analyst from Keenan Vision, predicts the value of goods and services sold over the Internet using auction technology will be $129 billion by 2002.

Knexa has now repositioned itself to target the buying and selling of business-related knowledge. David H. Brett, president and founder of Knexa, is convinced that in today's fast paced and dynamic economy where time is a valuable commodity, the more targeted approach in communications will reach the right audiences at the right time. Knexa's new slogan, Knowledge for Business, will begin to target specific categories in business and will ensure that communications initiatives reach these audiences. Knexa.com enables businesses to market their valuable knowledge content on the Internet. A survey of Knexa's registered users indicates that 80 percent seek or are interested in offering business knowledge.

"Providing knowledge services to business is nothing new," Brett acknowledges. "Knexa is taking advantage of the fact that more and more of these services are being provided online at a time of increasing demand in the market. We're applying the eBay concept to knowledge products in digital form. It could be anything from a report to an account of best practices for a company – anything that is used to convey knowledge in digital form. The ultimate vision I have for Knexa is to become the market place for intangibles of all kinds. That would extend into intel-

Certain knowledge might have a very limited shelf life.

lectual property such as licenses, business processes, and patents. I also see it moving into the area of human capital in which people are engaging in online consulting. As broadband services become more available, we can become an exchange for people as well as their ideas and knowledge. The vision is to encompass all of those intangibles eventually."[21]

This leads inevitably to the question: what exactly is knowledge and how can it be packaged to trade on an open market? "Knowledge is experiential information, intelligence applied through and gained from experience," say Joseph Pine and James Gilmore in *The Experience Economy*.[22]

Add Thomas Davenport and Lawrence Prusak in *Working Knowledge*: "Knowledge is a fluid mix of framed experience, values, contextual information, and expert insight that provides a framework for evaluating and incorporating new experiences and information. It originates and is applied in the minds of knowers in organizations. In organizations, it often becomes embedded not only in documents or repositories but also in organizational routines, processes, practices and norms."[23]

The value of knowledge can be subject to a number of variables such as time and the credibility of the seller. Certain knowledge might have a very limited shelf life, such as computer programming hints. Insight on how to set up an Internet business in China might be worth a fortune on one day and nothing the next, depending on changes in government policy. The dynamic pricing capability of an online auction is perfectly suited to knowledge markets as valuations are free to fluctuate.

The Internet is just the enabler and connector. Forget e-commerce, intellectual commerce – i-commerce – is what matters. As one observer phrased it, the worldwide web is "a place where you can empty your head and fill your wallet!" The other implication might be that the firm as a concrete place is replaced by knowledge exchanges. The exchanges become the multipliers, the springboards to release the value potential of human brains. Firms become museums or prisons afflicted by inefficiency in utilizing human talent.

COMPASS LINKS

www.knexa.com
www.knownet.org
www.bontis.com
www.interesting.org

TAKING BEARINGS

- What knowledge markets are you and your organization involved in?
- How could you auction your own knowledge?
- Are you allowed to trade your own knowledge?

UNSEEN WEALTH CREATORS

So, where does all this leave us? Most obviously, it makes it clear that it is no longer primarily investments by individuals and businesses in more physical assets, such as factories, machines, office buildings, farmland, and mineral resources, which are driving economic growth. Today, investments are in more intellectual, organizational, institutional, and reputational assets. They have to be.

"Some academic theorists and analysts believe that the high stock values seen in today's equity markets are attributable principally if not entirely to the substantial build-up of hidden intangible capital that is not reported in company returns, or elsewhere in government statistics," notes a report by the Brookings Task Force entitled *Unseen Wealth*.[24] It goes on to add a caution. "However, the contention that the gap is attributable entirely to unbooked 'intellectual capital' is now largely discredited as too simplistic and that the influence of other factors, such as rising returns to book equity and a fall in the cost of equity must be taken into account."

Indeed they must. But even if you don't attribute the entire change to intellectual capital, you're still left with the unavoidable conclusion that something significant has happened to the way enterprises are valued. It could be that the availability of venture capital, for example, has shifted the goalposts. But what does this suggest? Money is no longer the scarce resource it was. The scarce resource in the knowledge economy is – know–how, know–who and knowing. Today, the VC money is chasing thought models, the ideas and the people who know how to make things happen. At the very least, even if returns to book value are increasing, then this suggests that the old ways of assessing value and return on investment need recalibrating.

Evidence is massing. In their work on the physical and intellectual capital of Austrian banks, Ante Pulic and Manfred Bornemann concluded that the "rise of efficiency in intellectual capital is the simplest, cheapest and most secure way to ensure sustainable success."[25] Pulic's work at the Austrian Intellectual Capital Research Center has championed the use of the Value Added Intellectual Coefficient (VAIC) tool to monitor and measure how intellectual capital creates value – and how much. "The present accounting system remains closely tied to capital employed and financial capital flows, still lacking relevant information on the performance of intangible resources," laments Pulic.[26]

Interesting research also comes from Mitchell Williams of the University of Calgary. He considered whether a company's intellectual capital performance and its propensity to disclose its intellectual capital practices were related. His conclusion is thought provoking: "There may indeed be some form of association between a firm's intellectual capital performance and related disclosure practices … when intellectual capital is perceived to be too high by management this could be seen as an advantage to the company and something that should not be disclosed for fear of signaling competitors to the advantage and opportunity achieved by the entity. Firms having achieved a high level of intellectual capital performance may fear that given the ease and speed of transferability of intellectual capital, excessive intellectual capital disclosure could in fact place it at a disadvantage by indicating to its competitors markets, employees and processes they could utilize in their own operations."[27]

Baruch Lev remains one of the most powerful voices in charting knowledge economics. Two important findings from his research have been influential. First, he suggests that companies which invest heavily in knowledge creation, are more likely to be valued above their book value than those that don't.[28] So, for example, the gap between the value of Microsoft's physical assets and its market value is much larger than, say, a traditional manufacturer. The additional value is a measure of Microsoft's potential to create wealth in the future. Sure, it may be influenced by other factors as well, but the basic fact remains.

A second, practical breakthrough came with Lev's knowledge index, by which stock market values are discounted by reference to normalized earnings and returns on the physical and financial capital employed.[29] Although not an absolute measure, the resulting estimate of intangible capital takes account of cyclical factors and "irrational exuberance," and provides a useful tool for intercompany comparison purposes. It offers a more insightful measure.[30]

This points to another significant shift in the knowledge economy – changes in what is perceived as valuable. Value, as the thought-leadership battle shows, is in the eye of the beholder. But knowledge in its raw state is seldom valuable. Knowledge must be leveraged to create value. As Thomas Henry Findley observed: "The great end of knowledge is not knowledge but action."

This takes us to our next destination in the knowledge economy: the drivers of value.

COMPASS LINKS

www.measuring-ip.at
www.baruch-lev.com
www.bontis.com
www.nimcube.com

TAKING BEARINGS

- How large is the gap in value between your physical assets and your company's market value?
- Is it above or below the average in your industry?
- How does it compare to Microsoft's?

References

Notes

1 Kurtzman, Joel, "An interview with W Brian Arthur," *Strategy & Business*, Second Quarter 1998
2 Kurtzman, Joel, "An interview with Paul Romer," *Strategy & Business*, First Quarter 1997
3 Lucier, Charles Lucier & Torsilieri, Janet, "The end of overhead," *Strategy & Business*, Second Quarter 1999
4 www.kee-inc.com
5 Bureau of Economic Analysis, National Income and Product Accounts, Table 1.1.
6 Kurtzman, Joel, "An interview with Paul Romer," *Strategy & Business*, First Quarter 1997
7 Management Review, 1999
8 Slywotzky, Adrian, "How Digital is Your Company?" *Fast Company*, February 1999
9 Extracting value from innovation is also focused on by Patrick H Sullivan in his work – which includes the book, *Profiting from Intellectual Capital*, and also funding the collaborative intellectual property ICM Group established in 1995 in Berkeley, California. Stories on realizing value from IC assets and the place of patent assets in the corporate landscape can be found in Suzanne Harrison and Julie Davies' *Edison in the Boardroom*.
10 Skyrme, David, *Capitalizing on Knowledge*, Butterworth Heinemann, Oxford, 2001. Skyrme offers an interesting model of readiness for k-business.
11 *Washington Post*, April 29, 2000.
12 Mayo, Andrew, *The Human Value of Enterprise*, Nicholas Brealey, London, 2001
13 *The Intangible Economy: Impact And Policy Issues*, Report of the European High Level Expert Group on the Intangible Economy, 2000
14 *The Intangible Economy: Impact And Policy Issues*, Report of the European High Level Expert Group on the Intangible Economy, 2000
15 Wallman, Steven and Blair, Margaret, *Unseen Wealth*, Brookings Institute, 2001
16 Williams, S Mitchell, "Relationship between board

structure and a firm's intellectual capital performance in an emerging economy," unpublished paper
17 Nakamura, Leonard I, Federal Reserve Bank of Philadelphia
18 Manasco, Britton, "Leading companies focus on managing and measuring intellectual capital," *Knowledge Inc.*, undated
19 KM World 2000 conference September 2000
20 The Delphi Group forecasts that within five years, what it calls, "person-to-person e-commerce" will total $5 billion a year.
21 Interview, bizreport.com, September 28, 2000
22 Pine, Joseph, & Gilmore, James, *The Experience Economy*, Harvard Business School Press, 1999
23 Davenport, Thomas, & Prusak, Lawrence, *Working Knowledge*, Harvard Business School Press, Boston 1998
24 Unseen Wealth, Report of the Brookings Task Force on Understanding Intangible Sources of Value, Washington, 2001
25 Pulic, Ante & Bornemann, Manfred, "The physical and intellectual capital of Austrian banks," www.measuring-ip.at
26 Pulic, Ante, "MVA and VAIC analysis of randomly selected companies form FTSE 250," Austrian Intellectual Capital Research Center, April 2000
27 Williams, S Mitchell, "Is a company's intellectual capital performance and intellectual capital disclosure practices related?," unpublished paper, November 2000
28 Lev, Baruch, "The boundaries of financial reporting and how to extend them", SEC Symposium, Washington DC, April 1996
29 Lev, Baruch, "Seeing is believing," *CFO Magazine*, February 1999
30 Bontis, Nick, "An explorative study that develops measures and models," *Management Decision*, 36, 2, 1998

Changing
the Nature of Value

One man's treasure is another
man's worthless mystery.

WHAT IS VALUABLE?

Some time before 1000 BC in China, it was decided that trade could be improved through the introduction of a common currency. The currency that was selected was the cowrie shell. "Before coins were invented in China, cowrie shells were used as money," says Joe Cribb in *Money: From Cowrie Shells to Credit Cards*. Payments of cowries as rewards are described in inscriptions on ancient Chinese bronzes of the second millennium BC. Chinese archaeologists excavating tomb sites of the Shang period (sixteenth to eleventh centuries BC) have dug up large numbers of money cowries, often tied together in strings.

Other things which have been used as money include, according to Glyn Davies' *A History of Money*, amber, beads, drums, eggs, feathers, gongs, hoes, ivory, jade, leather, mats, nails, oxen, pigs, quartz, rice, salt, vodka, yarns and salt. Indeed, cowrie shells were still used as currency in Nigeria within living memory.

Today, few of us would be impressed by a man flaunting his cowrie shells. Our understanding of what is valuable evolves as the world changes. What is valuable changes over time. That is the nature of value though what is truly valuable – oxygen, water, warmth – is often not regarded as such.

Financial value pertains to scarce resources. In themselves, pieces of paper and metal coins are worthless. But money is valuable because it allows us to obtain other things. Every country in the world goes to great lengths to ensure its currency is rationed. (When it is not, the currency is devalued – as happened in Germany after WW1.)

The downside of financial value is that it can blind us. King Midas eventually turned himself into gold. Sometimes in the business world, deals which appear to be driven by finance are actually driven by more complex and intangible forces. Look, for example, at the world of mergers and alliances. At a superficial level such commercial endeavors are financial agreements for financial ends. In reality, however, alliances are about maximizing flow of knowledge and the value of knowledge. Alliances which don't work often concentrate on maximizing money rather than knowledge.

Andrew Inkpen from Arizona's Thunderbird School of International Management argues that "the formation of an alliance is an acknowledgement that an alliance partner has useful knowledge." According to Inkpen, success in sharing knowledge in alliances is related to two issues: how accessible the knowledge is and how effective the organizations are in acquiring knowledge. Alliance knowledge accessibility is, he suggests, driven by four issues. These are partner protectiveness (companies which were once competitors may find it difficult to switch to co-operation); trust between partners ("as trust increases and mutual partner understanding develops, alliance knowledge should become more accessible"); "knowledge tacitness" (explicit knowledge is, by its very nature, easier to communicate than tacit knowledge); and the history of the relationship between the companies.

According to Inkpen, effective acquisition of knowledge requires flexible learning objectives; leadership commitment; "no performance myopia" (Inkpen notes that alliance partners often measure effectiveness solely in financial terms and there is confusion between short and long term objectives; as well as between learning and financial measures); and cultural alignment. "As alliances increasingly become a fact of life in the business environment, exploiting the learning potential of alliances will become more important," Inkpen concludes. "By bringing together different firms with unique skills and capabilities, alliances can create powerful learning opportunities. However, without active management of the learning process and an understanding of the nature of alliance knowledge, many of these opportunities will remain unexploited. Properly managed, alliances can yield new and valuable insights that can lead to tangible performance improvements."

The point is that value does not necessarily lie where it is assumed to lie. The dynamics of value are usually about a lot more than money.

Move on three thousand years from cowrie shells to the summer of 2000. It is an August morning in London's Soho.

Though it is still only 8 a.m., outside one particular office building there is a huddle of people handing out business cards to all who enter or leave. Some have even ventured inside to disperse their cards to as many people as possible. This is the HQ of the Internet company Boo.com. The people handing out business cards with something approaching abandon are headhunters. They know that Boo.com is about to become the first big name European dot-com casualty. In an hour or two, its people will be looking for jobs. They want them.

By lunchtime on the day of Boo's demise, five of Soho's trendiest watering holes were invaded by search firm suits looking to sign up Boo personnel for prospective clients. One headhunter put £5000 behind the bar just to attract Boo employees.

Boo.com was fated – and feted – from the start. Boo and its Swedish founders Ernst Malmsten, Kajsa Leander and Patrik Hedelin, encountered technical problems early on – the launch had to be delayed – and never really took off.

As the value of the company disappeared; the value of the people sustained.

The quality of the consumer's experience failed to match the marketing hype. Having raised $135 million at the beginning of 1999, by May 2000 Boo was going bankrupt with reportedly $70 million in liabilities. Much of the money was blitzed on Boo's marketing campaign. Boo.com's spectacular collapse marked the end of innocence in the European dot-com sector.

What was left? What was valuable amid the commercial ruins? Not much you could touch. Boo's computers and office equipment were all leased, so were its premises. It had some stock in warehouses in Cologne and Kentucky. Its proprietary software – the fulfilment and delivery system – was sold to another London-based Internet company, Bright Station. The credibility of the company's founders was in tatters.

And then, there were Boo's people. As the value of the company disappeared, the value of the people was sustained. The crowd of headhunters got their prey. The programmers and the like were quickly snapped up. Managers who had conspicuously failed – in traditional terms – fared equally well. Failure no longer tarnishes. Failing so gloriously with an iconic Internet brand brings a certain kudos. The founders write a book – *Boo.Hoo: a dot com story from conception to catastrophe.* The 400 employees vanish with their insights into new jobs.

The final remnant of the once celebrated company was the brand name. Boo may have achieved fame for all the wrong reasons but Manhattan-based Fashionmall bought the rights – for an alleged $550,000 – to Boo's website *www.boo.com* believing that brand recognition outweighs negative publicity. The US company saw the infamous brand as a way into the European market

Because their assets are mostly intangible – things such as domain names and trademarks – Internet companies can be liquidated quickly but usually only to other companies which value such assets. Like Boo, dot-coms often don't own their premises, or have much in the way of inventory. Many lease their office furniture and computer equipment. Their true value lies in their people, knowledge recipes and in their brands. For many dot-coms, the rest is mere decoration.

The lesson of Boo is that, in the knowledge economy, value is attributed to different things – intangibles – than in the economy of the past – tangibles. Finance is still important, but it is not the be-all-and-end-all of what constitutes value. Value and what is valuable changes and is changing constantly as well as rapidly. Yesterday's gold might be today's fool's gold. Sustainable values might be more valuable tomorrow.

COMPASS LINKS	TAKING BEARINGS
www.europa.eu.int	• What is of value to you?
www.boo.com	• What do you consider of value in your organization?
	• How do you calculate its value?
	• How can you make it even more valuable?
	• What is the exit value of ideas?
	• What will be the new currency in the trade for thoughts?
	• What values shape value?

THE MARKET IN TALENT

As we have seen, thought recipes are valuable. Business thought models are valuable. And, as Boo.com shows, people are valuable. The market for talent – brain potential – has never been more intense.

This is ironic given the way in which many companies downsized in the early 1990s. Times change. "There will continue to be, for the foreseeable future, greater demand than supply of the best people – the most knowledgeable, skilled, innovative, experienced, entrepreneurial, creative, risk taking super talent," says Bruce Tulgan author of *Winning the Talent Wars* and co-founder of the think tank Rainmaker Thinking. "Every business leader and manager in every organization I talk with says that they are spending more time and energy and money on recruiting at all levels."[1]

A global battle for brains is emerging with global knowledge migration set to increase. This is creating a new tribe of knowledge nomads.

The value of talent is not altered by recession or downturn. In a 2001 update to its 1997 survey, which launched the war for talent debate, McKinsey & Company researchers surveyed 6,900 managers at 56 large and midsize US companies. They found that 89 percent of those surveyed thought it is more difficult to attract talented people now than it was three years ago, and 90 percent thought it is now more difficult to retain them. Just seven percent of the survey's respondents strongly agreed that their companies had enough talented managers to pursue all or most promising business opportunities.

According to McKinsey, demographic and social changes have played a growing role in this trend. In the US and most other developed nations, the supply of 35 to 44 year olds is shrinking. And many of the best-trained people entering the workforce are not bound for large traditional companies. In 2000, for example, 30 percent of US MBA graduates preferred to work for a start-up or a small business. And the percentage of computer science and electrical engineering graduates who went to smaller companies rather than more established ones has risen to 37 percent, from 22 percent in the 1980s.

The 2001 update also found that the companies doing the best job of managing their talent deliver far better results for shareholders. Companies scoring in the top quintile of talent-management practices outperform their industry's mean return to shareholders by 22 percentage points. Talent management isn't the only driver of such performance but, says McKinsey, it is clearly a powerful one.

Senior managers report that "A players" – the best 20 percent or so of managers – raise operational productivity, profit, and sales revenue much more than average performers do. In one manufacturing company surveyed, the best plant managers increased profits by 130 percent; in an industrial-services firm, the best operations managers achieved increases of 80 percent. (The worst managers in both companies brought no improvement.) The senior executives in the update survey thought top performers deserve pay 42 percent higher than that of average performers. The researchers found that paying an additional 40 percent to hire an A player could yield an overall return of 100 percent or more in a single year.

Despite the potential impact of top performers, both the 1997 study and the update revealed a gap between awareness of the talent issue and an effective response to it. Only 14 percent of the managers in the new survey (as opposed to 23 percent in 1997) strongly agreed that their companies attract highly talented people. Only three percent of the respondents to both surveys strongly agreed that their companies develop talent quickly and effectively.

The other side to the demographic coin is that the executive talent that's out there isn't getting any younger. At a time when the cult of youth may be unsustainable, many veterans are ready to get out. Changes in attitude – and high returns on their investments in recent years – make retirement an increasingly attractive option.

Companies not only have to find the right people, they have to keep them. If people are valuable, attracting and retaining the right people is ever more important. This is made doubly difficult by the increase in part-time work and the rise of knowledge nomads, free agents flitting from project to project. The average proportion of self-employed people, often referred to as knowledge nomads, in the Group of Seven countries is estimated to be 11 percent by Hamish McRae. In the UK this figure is already 15 per cent.

A monopsony is a situation in which there is only one buyer. It is as inefficient a situation as a monopoly. Monopsonies existed once in the employment world, but no more. As Mick Cope puts it in his book, *Know Your Value*, there are an awful lot of buyers, if you visualize your talent and explore new delivery logistics.[2]

Talent has a price. It is now commonplace for smaller companies to pay out bounties to attract the right people. This was once the preserve of large organizations – typically consulting firms who have been waving dollars in the air for years.

Another approach comes from Filtronic, which supplies infrastructure components to the mobile telecoms market. It acquired Maryland-based Sigtek Inc., a specialist in high-speed digital signal processing (DSP). The deal valued the US company at $20 million but there were strings attached. Filtronic aimed to ensure the 23 specialist engineers who worked for Sigtek would stick around. Only $4.7 million was paid upfront. The balance was scheduled for payment over the next four years, with the deferred element subject to an earn-out criteria based on the number and quality of engineers Sigtek managed to hold onto.

"Sigtek's business isn't particularly interesting to us," a senior executive at Filtronic told one reporter. "What we really wanted were people rather than a business and this deal is like recruiting 23 engineers." It makes sense. Filtronic, whose customers include Nokia, Motorola, and Ericsson as well as Philips and Lucent Technologies, has its eye trained on the 3G (third generation) mobile communications market where DPS is seen as a key emerging technology. Filtronic is betting that there won't be enough DPS technologists to go round and wants to lock in and retain its new employees.

The flow of perks and extras is becoming more extreme and lavish.

One side effect of all this is that the flow of perks and extras is becoming more extreme and lavish. Free underwear is among the perks being offered to staff at Salomon Smith Barney in return for their loyalty. The firm is offering staff a clothes allowance, which includes under garments; and is throwing in free toothbrushes. Salomon is also offering free gourmet meals for employees working late and complimentary laptop computers.

Perks are the new way companies hope to establish themselves as the employer of choice. In the war for staff retention, perks have become a battleground. But perks miss the point. In the end, employees don't stay loyal because a company provides a free massage service or manicure, concierge or casual dress code. They stay if they feel that the work and the pay do justice to their talents. They stay if they are valued and feel valued, and can leverage their talent. No amount of mollycoddling will change that basic fact. The talent war is a battle for respect as well as a battle to leverage human potential.

The combination of the rise in importance of talented people and greater emphasis on individuals taking responsibility for their own careers has, not surprisingly, brought a boom in the recruitment industry. Typical of the new breed is Wideyes which described itself as "a third generation, innovative, career-focused Internet recruitment company." Wideyes was founded in Sweden and has now merged into Jobline/Monster, one of the largest Internet-based talent providers. It captured 40 percent of the Swedish market within 40 days of its launch.

Careers and recruitment will increasingly be global in reach and ambition.

The eye-catching things about such a company are its global reach – knowledge jobs and work of today really are global; the bolt-on services the Internet now enables companies to provide; and the bravura feeling that people really are changing things.

Says Krister Hanner, co-founder and vice chairman of Wideyes: "It is a simple case of supply and demand – there are too many companies searching for the same gifted individuals. This has opened new opportunities to prospective employees, empowering them with choices beyond traditional benefits such as a good salary, car and bonus scheme. Wideyes has realised that these e-talent candidates want more and that traditional recruitment techniques will no longer be enough – hence the dawn of the third generation of recruitment."

Careers and recruitment will increasingly be global in reach and ambition. Companies like Monster.com can cover dozens of markets in the same global scalable database. Companies, with global recruitment requirements, can gain access to superior talent to maintain their competitive advantage.

It is not only a question of global reach. Increasingly, companies will outsource much of the recruitment process to speed it up. There is room for growth – only 8 percent of recruitment is now handled externally. Internet recruiting offers a bespoke web-based system to manage internal and external recruitment for corporations.

Typical of what is happening is the fact that Wideyes has also developed a partnership with SHL, the world's leading developer of psychometric testing software. It offers candidates the opportunity to create their emotional intelligence profile, which many industry commentators are suggesting, is more closely linked with success, than IQ. Emotional fit rather than intellectual fit is critical of networking. "Finding the right job now is no longer about who pays the most or which company looks best on your CV – candidates want a job that will enable them to fulfil their aspirations. It could be said that material rewards are not enough, emotional rewards are equally as important," explained Jonas Granstrom, then president of Wideyes. "Today's workforce is not so much about whether you have a degree from Oxbridge, but how well you respond to situations. The Internet has brought a more global economy, but it has not stopped developing. Candidates have to be flexible, able to read a situation and the reactions of their colleagues rapidly, and that requires emotional intelligence." Together with SHL, Wideyes developed an on-line test to help to highlight a candidate's emotional abilities – for example, a good listener could be a management consultant, a negotiator or a doctor. Elusive, yet critical, talent and releasing the potential of talent is another stopping off place in the quest to fully understand the emergent nature of intangible value.

> **Companies will outsource much of the recruitment process to speed it up.**

COMPASS LINKS
www.monster.com
www.rainmakerthinking.com

TAKING BEARINGS
- How do you attract people to your organization?
- What would attract you to another employer?
- How many buyers do you have for your talent?
- How close to your talent potential are you in your existing job position?
- Do you have a website to visualize your talent?

THE NEW POWER BROKERS

But worrying though demographics may be, far more significant is the simple fact that brains now represent the core value of business after business. People have the power and the potential. Human capital is a fact rather than a neat phrase. Power is still concentrated in the hands of the few talent clusters. Individuals inside and outside big corporations call the tune. Rogues rule.

In the outside world the new power brokers are people like Matt Drudge. For corporations the people to take notice of are people like Shawn Fanning. Fanning was a 19-year-old student who came up with a neat software program called Napster. It made it possible for individuals to trade pirate music tracks over the Internet and could shift the balance of power not only in the record industry but many other industries as well. Not surprisingly, the major record companies didn't like the idea and consulted their lawyers. Napster became embroiled in what could be a landmark legal case. Some have even suggested it could signal the death knell of copyright. IPR RIP?

Bright upstarts can now change the world.

Fanning is just one example of what big corporations are now up against. In less than ten months Napster had over ten million users. That's very fast growth even by Internet standards. To put it into perspective it took AOL over 10 years to accumulate 10 million users.

Bright upstarts can now change the world. Meanwhile, inside organizations power increasingly resides in the hands of the few. Bill Gates has observed that if 20 people were to leave Microsoft, the company would risk bankruptcy.

And their importance is set to grow. Kjell Nordström and Jonas Ridderstråle have labelled these key individuals as core competents. In a study by the Corporate Leadership Council, a "computer" firm recognized 100 core competents out of 16,000 employees; a "software" company had 10 out of 11,000; and a "transportation" group deemed 20 of its 33,000 employees as really critical. In other words, the percentage of core competents varied between 0.6 percent and 0.06 percent.[3]

"Core competents are increasingly a key competitive advantage," say Nordström and Ridderstråle in *Funky Business*. "Today, people hire organizations, rather than vice versa – organizations that are disposable rather than permanent. The stars are in charge. They have alternatives each and every minute of each and every day. Lose one and they will all say good-bye. Stars attract stars; losers pull in losers. We are all players in the great global attraction game – individuals, organizations and regions alike."[4]

Core competents are like the stars in old-fashioned movie studios. They call the shots. Movies are scripted to fit their looks, skills and aspirations. Now, organizations have to be shaped to fit the talents within.

One logical development from this is that movie agents are now eyeing the business world. If talented business people are stars in the corporate world why not treat them like stars? In the "attention economy" described by Tom Davenport, what could be more natural than focusing attention on previously unseen executive talent?

Leigh Steinberg is a sports star agent – and the model for Tom Cruise's character in the film, *Jerry Maguire*. "Show me the money" is Steinberg's unsophisticated but persuasive catchphrase.

It obviously works. His law firm, Steinberg & Moorad, represents more than 100 athletes and negotiates multi-million dollar deals for some of America's best known sports stars. Steinberg is now exploring ways of expanding his business to include negotiating on behalf of top business talent.[5]

Think where this might lead. A Mark McCormack figure may emerge as an agent for the world's top knowledge workers. Imagine a super team of executives all handled by McCormack. Think of the power they would possess, individually and as a group. In the sporting world, the arrival of agents like McCormack shifted the balance from the sports administrators to the sports talents. Thanks to McCormack and others, the prize money in tennis and golf went through the roof. Perhaps a similar transition is possible in the business world, with the star name knowledge workers calling the shots and the corporations doing what they are told.[6]

COMPASS LINKS
www.napster.com
www.funkybusiness.com

TAKING BEARINGS
- Where do you find an agent and broker for your knowledge potential?
- Could you become tomorrow's outsider, the person re-delineating an entire industry?
- Could your organization provide a structured spring-board for someone with an industry-changing thought-model?

PUTTING A PRICE ON TRUST

Thought recipes and thought models are valuable. Ideas are valuable. People are valuable. What else?

As we have seen in the story of Boo.com there is a value in brands – even brands which have never made any money and which are embedded in the public consciousness as glorious failures.

Branding used to be a statement of ownership. Brands were burned onto cattle. In Swedish the word for brand is the same as the word for fire. The brand was a visual, tangible, statement of ownership.

As you would expect, things are now a little less tangible. Thinking is based on values. Central to the notion of the value of the modern brand is the issue of trust, yet another abstract in this elusive mass of intangibles. Can the thinking of your business partner be trusted?

In the bright, fashionable, high-tech world of the new economy, the old-fashioned virtue of trust is an elusive quality. Trust is the bridge on which knowledge is travelling to be exchanged.

A survey of 200 UK internet users by the advertising agency Leo Burnett found that for all the millions spent on marketing, consumers still trust traditional company brands more than bright and shiny dot-coms. While name recognition is high, trust is stubbornly low. Lastminute.com was recognized by 84 percent of people but only trusted by 17 percent. In contrast, organizations such as the BBC, the retailer Boots, and the financial services company Prudential have a healthy reservoir of trust to fall back on.

"Trust is not conjured creatively," says Tony Cram, program director at the management college Ashridge. "The words 'Trust me' from a salesman you have never previously met are likely to achieve the exact opposite effect. Likewise for dot-coms, they cannot ask for immediate trust, it is earned by behavior over time. Trust is confidence in future behavior for both personal and brand relationships. We look for patterns of behavior and trust grows where we see consistency. Time is clearly important, and the most trusted brands – Heinz, Kelloggs, Cadbury – have all shown their consistent performance over many years. On the web, both Dell and Amazon are working progressively towards joining these brands."

The consulting firm Bain & Company has led the way in exploring the field of customer loyalty and has now undertaken two years of research into e-loyalty. Bain's Frederick Reichheld and Phil Schefter simply conclude: "Price does not rule the web; trust does."

"Without the glue of loyalty, even the best-designed e-business model will collapse," they note. This explains why CEOs at the cutting edge of e-commerce – from Michael Dell, to eBay's Meg Whitman – care deeply about customer retention. Loyalty, say Reichheld and Schefter, is an economic necessity. "Acquiring customers on the Internet is enormously expensive, and unless those customers stick around and make lots of repeat purchases over the years, then profits will remain elusive."

They cannot ask for immediate trust, it is earned by behavior over time.

Nowhere is the importance of trust better illustrated than in the increasingly fraught world of online banking. Online banking is a great idea. The cost savings are clear. No need for all that bricks and mortar in expensive downtown locations. And online banking brings better, more efficient, instant service whenever customers want it. They can reorder their finances at the dead of night when they are holidaying on a distant beach. There is only one problem: the latest research suggests that when it comes to money, consumers prefer bricks to clicks.

For the moment at least, online banking appears to make sense only to banks. Trust is generally notable by its absence. A survey, commissioned by identity consultancy, Henrion, Ludlow & Schmidt (HLS), found that only seven percent of people trust online banks, compared with 75 percent who place more trust in bricks and mortar banks. A thoroughly dispirited fourteen percent trust neither.

In the United States, this lack of trust is manifest in a reaction against online banking. According to consultants, McKinsey & Company, "physical" banking is on the increase – up from 54 transactions per household in 1993 to 62 in 1998. More than 80 percent of customers visit a branch once a month and physical bank outlets generate 80 percent to 90 percent of new deposit, investment and loan accounts. Online broker, Charles Schwab, plans a 15 percent to 20 percent increase in physical outlets over the next few years. (In a neat twist, many of these will be in closed-down retail bank premises.)

"It is significant that only seven percent of people trust the new Internet banks more than the traditional bricks and mortar ones. The findings have far-reaching implications for those responsible for creating lasting and credible online brands, particularly given the recent collapse of high profile dot-com start ups," says HLS partner, Chris Ludlow. "Trust is essential when building brands, especially in the financial services industry where credibility and security are paramount. Given the new ways of communicating, made possible through advances in technology, it is tempting to believe that brands can now be built overnight. Clearly this is not the case."

Banks need to think harder about the branches they close.

So, how do you build trust? A potential way forward in the banking world comes from the McKinsey consultants Matthias M. Bekier, Dorlisa K. Flur, and Seelan J. Singham. They suggest that banks have to exercise a little more guile in their strategies. Market segments have to be targeted and outlets restructured (one bank redesigned a branch as a coffee bar to attract the affluent young set). And banks need to think harder about the branches they close – small customer numbers may not necessarily equate to low value. They also need to help customers "migrate" to new branches when their local one is closed, perhaps by moving a popular teller from the old to the new. And they need to think positively about such things as outsourcing branches to supermarkets or post offices, leasing spare banking space to retail outlets or franchising their branches.

The trouble is that though trust is a simple concept, it is incredibly difficult to build. One approach that adds to trust is to increase the transparency and visibility of intangibles by rating intellectual capital. According to research at the University of Gothenburg in Sweden, this reduces uncertainty and the volatility of stock performance and, consequently, acts as a kind of trust insurance for intangibles.[7]

"There is more to it than time alone," says Ashridge's Tony Cram. "Counter-intuitively, trust seems to build faster with a series of short interactions, rather than a single intense experience. DHL has demonstrated that regularity and frequent touch points can build trust in a shorter timescale. Similarly, it is no coincidence that the most trusted retailers are those which are visited the most frequently.

"Contact variety is also a factor in building relationships. The BBC can be experienced on radio, TV, through books, magazines and on the web. Audiences may write, telephone or email reactions. Banks began leaking trust when they encouraged customers to use external ATMs to replace over the counter contact. The same is happening in the United States with the major gasoline brands encouraging customers to swipe a card on the pump instead of paying inside the filling station. Automation is not in itself brand damaging, but it is difficult to build a trusting relationship if the contact is one-dimensional. This is why leading dot-coms like the educational toy e-tailer, Smarterkids.com, are offering telephone contact points, and text boxes on their screens for typed dialogue."

How the brands of today react to their current problems will have a great bearing on whether they will become brands of tomorrow. But it is only through trust that the brands of tomorrow will succeed.

COMPASS LINKS

www.intellectualcapital.se
www.valuestech.com
www.4Dbranding.com

TAKING BEARINGS

- Why do people trust your enterprise?
- What are the dominant characteristics of you brand?
- How do you cultivate your brand?
- How do you rate the trustworthiness of your business?

RELATIONSHIP CAPITAL

The astonishing performance of shares in dot-coms early in 2000 is a key example of the way in which old criteria used by investors to value companies have broken down in new knowledge-intensive industries. Tangible assets are only part of the story – and often an insignificant one – for an Internet start-up or biotech company. According to C.J. Choi and A. Karamanos of Cambridge University's Judge Institute of Management, far more important are a company's existing and potential connections with key stakeholders. A biotechnology firm's value may largely be a matter of its relationship with certain leading scientists and the standing this relationship gives it among other scientists. So, the next source of value is relationships.

The two Cambridge academics suggest that by combining ideas from stakeholder theory and categorization theory, a company's value can be shown to be a function of the network of connections it makes. This approach looks not just at the position of a company in its network of stakeholders but also at the positions of its associates in theirs. For example, some research scientists are renowned and highly respected in their field while others remain relatively unknown among colleagues. A biotechnology firm that forms relationships with high-profile scientists will itself have a higher profile in the scientific world than one that works with less well-known researchers. This higher profile among a key group of stakeholders translates into higher value.

This approach is intriguing – by assessing the level of reputation of people associated with these new companies in their own fields (rather than the one in which the company operates) Choi and Karamanos attempt to put a "value" on the intangible assets of the company. In other words, the individual standing of the people within a firm translates to the firm itself. While this might not replace some existing methods of financial valuation, it does represent a new approach to an old problem. Although not a way of calculating value quantitatively, the approach does yield a qualitative ranking of companies within a given sector. It is a kind of citation index for personal networking similar to the way a patent citation index is used for assessment of intellectual property.

The Cambridge duo are simply trying to make sense of another emergent area of incredible potential value: networks. Networks create what I call "relationship capital." Once again, there's nothing particularly new in this – in 1750 the Italian economist Ferdinando Galiani stated that "value is a relation between persons."

Networks work at two levels: corporate networks; and personal networks. (Or, in other words, structural and human capital.)

First there are corporate networks. Increasingly, companies are, as we will see when we explore organizational forms, little more than networks. They are institutionalized networks with (more or less) visible brands and structural capital.

Take Sun Microsystems, the networking giant which introduced the cross-platform Java technology. The company is one of Silicon Valley's legendary success stories. Founded in 1982 it has grown from a company with four employees to one employing 35,000 people, and generating annual revenues of over $15 billion today. It is a company driven by a vision: "The network is the computer." And the network is also the company. So much so, that CEO Scott McNealy has a dog named Network and made it the company mascot.

At a personal level, McNealy's enthusiasm for selling Sun systems extends to some high profile networking. Famously, he challenged Jack Welch, General Electric's celebrated CEO, to a round of golf. McNealy lost, but so impressed Welch that he received a place on the GE board.

Like many other corporations Sun has a formal organizational chart. And like many other companies it's hierarchical, pyramidal in shape, with delineated reporting lines. That's not how it works in practice, though. The real indicator of the *de facto* organizational structure within Sun is the email trail. Follow the emails and it is possible to trace the clusters of knowledge and power within the company. It is just a question of finding out who is getting the critical emails.

This is exactly how Scott McNealy found out about Java. When he kept coming across emails along the lines of "Java group meeting" he guessed something important was happening within Sun. Something that he ought to become more acquainted with. He was right.

"The network's the thing," says Ian Abell of the incubator Brainspark. "It's difficult to measure its value, so it is easily ignored, but there's immense untapped value in business networks everywhere.

While most business relationships remain transactional, the emerging network thinkers ask, 'What extra value lies in this relationship above and beyond the most obvious transactional exchange?'."

Brainspark's network embraces people with the original idea for a business, venture capitalists, and, increasingly, those in the corporate and consulting spheres. The appeal of such a network is that it potentially allows organizations to benefit from economies of scale as well as entrepreneurial inspiration. It is the best of all worlds.

"The capital we invest in start-up companies provides the basic fuel to drive their business. But there are a lot of people with money to invest. So, in addition, we offer an infrastructure to start-ups which gives the business credibility from day one. As the start-up is wooing employees, customers, strategic partners and investors they do so from the heart of an environment buzzing with creative excitement and commercial success. The partners are seduced by the combined aura of the companies we're incubating, not just the lone start-up

There's immense untapped value in business networks everywhere.

they are visiting," explains Brainspark's Abell. "That's just the start of our network approach. We are currently connecting more quality players into our network and striving to make the network even more boundaryless. For those brave enough, the transparent network approach offers enormous value opportunities. Innovation can be as simple as connecting disparate nodes and allowing other players to view and offer insights." The result is a spiral of networks and links, spreading virus-like through the corporate world.

Then there are personal networks.

Every individual knows the value of networking. Some networks, of course, open more doors than others. This explains the enduring appeal of exclusive clubs. Businesspeople have always been a clubable lot, but the networking-obsessed new economy spawns new possibilities.

A global economy demands global clubs. Reaching across national borders, they can provide access, instant introductions around the world and legitimacy. Creating a community is the Internet Holy Grail - and clubs are instant communities. It is no surprise, then, that they are being seized upon as the way forward.

Recent years have seen the rise of clubs for the digerati. First Tuesday offers a meeting place and market for Internet start-ups. It started life in October 1998 at the Alphabet Bar in Soho, when founders Julie Meyer, Mark Davies, Adam Gold and Nick Denton brought together 80 "friends" involved with creating new media companies. It perfectly captured the dot-com moment, and soon boasted 100,000 members. It was eventually sold to an Israeli investment group for a reported $50 million. The club for the unclubbable is now a business, too. Listed on the OFEX exchange, the Groucho Club – founded in 1984 for Fleet Street's literati – has a market capitalization of £6.44 million, and was even the target of a hostile take-over bid.

The club as business model appeals to others. Also hitting the club scene are leading business thinkers. Belonging to an intellectual network has cachet. Along with lucrative consultancy work, the club can be a potent way to leverage guru brand status. This strategy is epitomized by the Strategos Institute, part of Strategos, the consulting operation founded by Gary Hamel, visiting professor of London and Harvard Business Schools.

To the select few, Strategos offers membership of its Institute – "a consortium of successful companies who are addressing the most fundamental business challenge of our time." The Strategos Institute offers two levels of membership – general membership or full partner level. General members can participate in two of the four research streams the Institute is pursuing, while partners can participate in all four. Partnership has its privileges – a one-day workshop with Gary Hamel designed expressly for the company.

The club can be a potent way to leverage guru brand status.

Another impressive network is that created by the Global Business Network (GBN). Founded by scenario-planning guru and former Shell executive Peter Schwartz and four friends in 1987, the idea emerged around a pool table in a Berkeley, California, basement. The five co-founders envisioned a worldwide learning community of organisations and individuals. GBN's Explorers Club is there to help companies "transition from the old to the new economy."

Clubs are essentially communities. Networks, too, are communities. Communities encourage dialog and enable people to share experiences and knowledge. Look, for example, at the intellectual capital community initiated by Skandia at *www.iccommunity.com* or at the communities shaped by Dee Hock in the United States.

In a business world of ambiguity and alienation, communities offer a sense of belonging. Networks – nebulous though they may be – offer the only certainties around, a sense of legitimacy to balance the uncertainty of intangibles. Networks, therefore, offer personal and commercial potential value.

COMPASS LINKS

www.pentaclethevbs.com
www.sun.com
www.brainspark.com
www.chaordic.org
www.iccommunity.com

TAKING BEARINGS

- How do you relate to your professional community?
- How big is your personal network – hundreds or thousands?
- How much time do you dedicate to networking and alliances?
- How does your enterprising benefit from shaping, cultivating and growing alliances and networks?
- How do you visualize this networking in your accounting?

Notes

1 Interview

2 Cope, Mick, *Know Your Value*, ft.com, London, 2000

3 Competence encompasses knowledge, will and skill, including professional, social and commercial ability. It is knowledge intentions. A core competence is a competence of strategic importance for the company's business logic.

4 Nordström, Kjell, & Ridderstråle, Jonas, *Funky Business*, ft.com 2000

5 Webber, Alan M, "How to get them to show you the money," *Fast Company*, November 1998

6 Now in its early stages, Progress Europe might be such an effort.

7 Haar, Christian, & Sundelin, Daniel, "IC – a determinant of market value volatility," unpublished master's thesis 2000

Renaissance Perspectives

Enterprise and people are built
in the future not in the past.

RENAISSANCE ACCOUNTING

In the business world, we have sought to understand value through accounting. Fifteenth century Italy is the unlikely source for modern accounting. The Renaissance man usually acknowledged as the father of double-entry bookkeeping and, therefore, modern accounting is Fra Luca Pacioli (1447–1517), a protégé of the painter Piero della Francesca and a tutor to Leonardo da Vinci. Pacioli did not invent the method but was its first coherent and detailed champion. He brought together strands of thinking and created a systematic thought model for counting value.

To his study of mathematics, Pacioli brought religious vigor – he took the vows of the Franciscan Order. "The purpose of every merchant is to make an honest and legitimate profit for his living. Wherefore they must begin all their transactions in the name of God and put his holy name on every account," he avowed.

Our accounting systems remain locked in the old economy.

Helpfully for his popular appeal, Pacioli published his work in Italian rather than Latin to reach a wider commercial audience. Key to his philosophy was that mathematics had to be practical.

Pacioli's legacy to the world was encapsulated in the 1497 publication *Summa de Arithmetica, Geometrica, Proportioni et Proportionalita*. This detailed but rambling discourse on mathematics, geometry, and proportion includes a diversion to enable Pacioli to describe the "Venetian method," the basis of double-entry bookkeeping. Pacioli pursued this diversion to help out the business of one of his friends, the Duke of Urbino (to whom the book was dedicated) – "In order that the subjects of the most gracious Duke of Urbino may have complete instructions in the conduct of business, I have determined to go outside the scope of this work and add this most necessary treatise," he explains. This single section of Pacioli's masterpiece – "Particularis de Computis et Scripturis" – became hugely popular. Before long it was translated into Dutch, German, French, English, and Russian.

Pacioli's method enabled the commercial adventurers of the time to make financial sense of their investments and adventures. If longitude allowed them to know where they were and where they were going; accounting enabled them to keep track of their riches. It provided a code where none before had existed.

Pacioli's methods have, of course, been refined massively over 500 years. But the principles remain much the same. They were perhaps most significantly translated into the modern corporate context by Pierre du Pont (1870–1954) at the turn of the twentieth century. In 1902, he and his cousins, Coleman and Alfred, took control of the family explosives company, Du Pont. As the company treasurer, Pierre introduced a series of innovative financial measures and systems. In 1903, du Pont introduced return on investment as a measure of organizational performance and went on to devise a formula to compare the performance of various departments. Du Pont, aided by his deputy John Raskob, basically instilled professional vigor into corporate accounting and financial systems. (Prior to this, in the nineteenth century, cost accounting had been developed by J. Edgar Thomson at the Pennsylvania Railroad.)

One-hundred-year-old refinements to 500-year-old principles hardly reassure. The truth is that though values have changed, our accounting systems remain locked in the old economy. Twenty-first-century notions of value can not be usefully or accurately understood through fifteenth-century techniques, however robust they may be.

The financial reporting system so beloved of the modern corporate world does not work – or, perhaps more accurately, doesn't tell the full story, including the story of intangibles. "I find balance sheets increasingly irrelevant as they currently stand. We have to find a way to make them more relevant," says Alan Reid, KPMG's chairman of international consulting.[1] "Financial accounts are produced with limited objectives in mind," observes the British politician Lord Sainsbury.[2] And fulsome criticism comes from Robert Reich: "Members of the accounting profession, not otherwise known for their public displays of emotion, have fretted openly about how to inform potential investors of the true worth of enterprises whose value rests in the brains of employees. They have used the term 'goodwill' to signify the ambiguous zone on the corporate balance sheets between the company's tangible assets and the value of its talented people. But as intellectual capital continues to overtake physical capital as the key asset of the corporation, shareholders find themselves on shakier and shakier ground."

Accounting rules aim to record what has happened in specific transactions and thereby track the flows of assets into and out of a corporation. Under the accounting principles used in the US and in most developed countries, for resources to be considered "assets," they must be well-defined and separate from other assets, the firm must have effective control over them, it must be possible to predict the future economic benefits from them, and it must be possible to determine if their economic value has been impaired, and to what extent (through, say, depreciation or depletion).[3] Herein lies a problem. These criteria mean that the term "assets" is generally interpreted to mean property, plant, and equipment, financial assets, and purchased, identifiable intangible assets. In other words, if you can't nail an asset down, then it won't show up in the books.

Traditional accounting misses out so much. People are largely ignored. The resignation of a vital person will not even register in the accounts unless they are the CEO. Yet, as we have seen, individuals can hold huge amounts of power – knowledge power – in today's organizations. If a top software developer leaves even a company as big as Microsoft it is significant.

If you can't nail an asset down, then it won't show up in the books.

Nor do accounts take relationships into consideration. If a key account is lost, it is not mentioned. If a key salesman leaves he takes his network with him. This is not mentioned in traditional accounting.

Indeed, not only do standard accounts tell a partial story, they tell one which is written in a foreign language. While Pacioli wrote in Italian in search of a popular audience, modern accountants have no such interest in popular appeal. How many people really understand the meaning of "return on adjusted net asset value?" Not many. Often it is only the most attentive board member who can decipher the profusion of footnotes and comments, which cover all sorts of dark secrets.

There is more. The value of networks is not covered by standard accounting. The values of brands are only now being concluded in annual reports.

Opportunity costs are similarly ignored. We are measuring the wrong things. Take market share. This is one of the things companies have become preoccupied with. They measure it with great enthusiasm and dedicate resources to making sure they know exactly how they are performing along this single parameter. This is all well and good as a measure. Market share tells you how much of the pie you already have or would like to have. What it doesn't cover is the opportunity share, whether you can enlarge and create new business. Knowing where you are is of little use if you don't have any idea where you're going.

Look at what we did at Skandia. It was an insurance company. It could have continued to concentrate on market share. It could have followed Alfred Sloan's dictum that "the business of business is business" and taken a narrow view. The realization at the company was that growth comes from vigorously seeking out new market opportunities rather than calculating the market share of markets you're already in. The future never lies in the present. So we transformed Skandia from an old insurance company into an innovative financial service organization. We moved from recycling best practice to exploring what really were our best options.

The reality is that we become what we measure. Accounting is a tool for visualization, communication as well as navigation. Managers have been besotted with measurement ever since Frederick Taylor got out his stopwatch in the nineteenth century. These are great times for measurement enthusiasts. As MIT's John Hauser and consultant Gerald Katz have pointed out, there are metrics for virtually every aspect of corporate performance – from contingent sales forecasts to customer satisfaction, market share to net present value.[4] Hauser and Katz argue that metrics can be dangerous. Indeed, they can alter the entire behavior of management. "If a firm measures a, b, and c, but not x, y, and z, then managers begin to pay more attention to a, b, and c. Soon those managers who do well on a, b, and c are promoted or are given more responsibilities. Increased pay and bonuses follow," they write. The end-result is that "the firm gains core strengths in producing a, b, and c. The firm becomes what it measures."

If we know so little how can we make the right decisions for ourselves and our businesses? Answer: We can't. "As long as capital markets, individual managers and governments rely on historical cost accounting to make allocation and policy decisions to the extent that the accounts don't reflect the new drivers of wealth production that are important to consider, the accounts are simply wrong and policies not as enlightened as they might be," says Steven Wallman, formerly a commissioner of the US Securities and Exchange Commission. "Knowledge assets are going to be the primary drivers of wealth production." (This is further refined in a book co-authored by Wallman, *Unseen Wealth*.[5])

Built on 500-year-old principles it is, perhaps, little wonder that accounting struggles with the new world of knowledge economics. "There is a need to move to a new level in accounting, one that measures a company's momentum in terms of market position, customer loyalty etc," says the venture capitalist Bill Davidow.[6]

There is a need for a second renaissance of accounting, accounting for intellectual capital. In their work on intellectual capital, a trio of University of Calgary academics concluded: "The traditional accounting model is not designed for this new economy, consequently, either the accounting model itself will need to change or companies will need to provide supplemental disclosures in their annual reports."[7]

The question then is how, for example, do you identify and codify human potential? How do you put a book value on structural capital? How, indeed, do you quantify the impact of human imagination? Under the current system, you don't. This does not mean it can't be done. It simply means that the current accounting system is inadequate. "If you can visualize it, you can measure it, and if you can measure it you can manage it," says Gordon Petrash, former director of intellectual capital at Dow Chemicals.[8]

Work is underway. The Financial Accounting Standard Board (FASB) in the United States, the Danish cabinet, and the IASB are among those shaping recommendations, guidelines, rules and software solutions to these issues.[9] Now Edmund Jenkins of the FASB argued in May 2001 that forward looking information regarding intangibles should be voluntarily disclosed outside corporate financial statements. This is moving towards Skandia's approach in the early 1990s to its IC supplements and close to the guidelines on IC accounting publishing by the Danish government in 2000. In October 2001 the SEC Chief Harvey Pitt was determined to overhaul the Nation's outdated system of financial reporting. Realization is dawning that accounting is concerned with costs as an internal information issue while value is an external information issue and intellectual capital about future earnings potential.

COMPASS LINKS
www.brookings.edu
www.fasb.org
www.iasb.org.uk
www.efs.dk/icaccounts
www.sec.gov/news/speech.html

TAKING BEARINGS
- What intangibles do you feature in your annual report?
- What are the implications of the new IASB rules for your accounting practice?
- How much do you understand and practice the concept of opportunity share rather than market share?
- How do you calculate opportunity costs for your intangibles?

THE INTANGIBLE GAP

The deficiencies in the accounting system explain a lot of the discrepancies we see occurring with stock market valuations.

The economist Robert Hall has analyzed the rather large discrepancy that has developed in the last decade or so between the value being assigned to firms by the financial markets and the value recorded on their books. He concludes that this empirical fact can only be reconciled with financial theories about how stocks are valued if "corporations own substantial amounts of intangible capital not recorded in the sector's books or anywhere in government statistics."[10]

It is like an iceberg emerging. Traditional reporting revealed only the tip of the iceberg. With a real iceberg, the part that shows above the water line is usually somewhere between one seventh and one tenth of the total volume -- the same goes for most knowledge intensive organizations. The book value versus the market value on the New York stock exchange is about one seventh of the whole.[11] In the case of Microsoft the market value was 30 times the book value. This shows one of the accounting paradoxes of today – that we have a very good descriptive system for financial capital (f-capital) but a very weak one for invisible and intellectual capital (i-capital).

The gap is transparent but widening. In the United States especially it has been growing since the middle of the 1980s thanks to the growth in investment in intangibles. According to Leonard Nakamura, chief economist of the Federal Reserve Bank of Philadelphia, the gross investment in intangibles is at least $1 trillion every year and the capital stock of intangibles is more than $5 trillion.[12]

Look at the case of Disney. In the summer of 2000, the company had a market capitalization of some $117 billion. Its stock totaled around $83 billion and the firm also

Traditional reporting revealed only the tip of the iceberg.

had about $34 billion in outstanding liabilities for a total market capitalization of $117 billion. But on the books, the firm had only $43.7 billion in assets. This total included some $11.3 billion worth of recognized intangible assets. But apparently the financial markets felt that Disney had more like $85 billion in intangibles – almost eight times the recognized book value of such assets.[13] Similarly, Sprint Corporation had total market capitalization (total liabilities at book value plus market value of equity) of $60.2 billion in early August, 2000, compared with $39 billion in book assets, which included $9.6 billion in recognized intangibles. Here again, the financial markets apparently thought that Sprint had nearly $31 billion worth of intangibles, more than three times what its balance sheet shows.[14]

Tangible assets are often a very small proportion of the market value of a corporation. In the case of Ericsson or SAP, tangible assets form only about 5 percent of the value. The question needs to be asked – who is in charge of the other 95 percent?

Intellectual assets or intellectual capital is where the volatility lies. Yet, it is with such knowledge assets that the potential for sustained earnings often lies rather than in the fixed capital. The collapse in values is driven by limited insights into intangibles.

Disney is especially interesting. Much of the credit for its success in recent years must go to Michael Eisner – one of a new breed of intellectual capitalists. Eisner's name may be filed under entertainment, but his great achievement is to have brought order to the creative chaos that was Disney. He brought new perspective to the company that allowed it to harness previously unrecognized potential.

Eisner's insight was that Disney is in the family entertainment business in all its manifestations. It wasn't just a movie company or a theme park operator. Eisner effectively redefined Disney, widening its perspective and ambition. He forgot about declining market share and unveiled new opportunities. He galvanized the company into action. Its waning innovative powers were re-discovered. The Disney brand was stretched to encompass a mountain of merchandising, stores (10 in 1988 have mushroomed to more than 600 generating sales of over $1 billion), books, videos, games, movies and theme parks. Eisner took intellectual capital and packaged it into new products. He proved adept at maximizing the profit potential of Disney's glorious back catalogue. A new generation got to know Disney and, so long as the movies were in people's minds, merchandise could be sold. The past was neatly repackaged for the future.

> **Return on equity or return on total assets, become much less useful in intangibles-intensive firms.**

There is more to it than cashing in on something you already have, however unrealized and intangible it may be. Studies (especially by Stern's Baruch Lev) show that firms in key growth industries (high-tech, life-sciences, and business-services sectors) tend to have high ratios of spending on R&D relative to sales, and, in turn, firms with high levels of spending on R&D tend to have high market to book ratios. Research has shown that firms that make the greatest investments in the education and training of their workforce have above average productivity and financial performance.[15]

Based on such figures, Baruch Lev has argued that the U.S. ought to move toward full capitalization of R&D expenses. Unfortunately, his proposals are still considered highly controversial.

The reality is that commonly used performance measures, such as return on equity or return on total assets, become much less useful in intangibles-intensive firms. Similarly, the "human capital" assets of firms — the stocks of skills, competencies, and know-how in a company, and the resources being expended to renew and expand them – are outside the visible spectrum of information that is typically available to investors. It simply doesn't show up on the financial radar. What investors are left with is guesswork. Guesswork can be expensive. In other words, sentiments are no substitute for fundamental insights into intellectual capital.

The lack of clear, quantifiable, and comparable information about intangible-intensive companies tends to encourage selective disclosure of inside information to key investors, making it easier for insiders to gain at the expense of outsiders and small investors. Sears, Roebuck, and Dow Chemical for example, have been trying to develop models that would show the link that they believe exists from employee satisfaction, to customer loyalty, to intellectual properties, to profit. They have spent years refining their data capture mechanisms. At the same time, no American company has gone public with IC supplements to its accounts unlike in Sweden and Denmark.

The ultimate goal of measurement, accounting, and information reporting systems in business enterprises and at the level of industries and national economies is to enable executives and policy makers to make better resource allocation decisions. Are enough resources going into employee training and development relative to purchases of new equipment and software, for example? Are investors willing to put new capital into worthy new business ventures that are intangibles intensive, at a reasonable cost of capital? Should governments provide stronger tax incentives to encourage even more investments in intangibles? Should governments invest in attracting foreign human capital?

What we need now is a new system, or at least a parallel one to supplement the existing financial measures. What we currently have is a one-dimensional co-ordinate – corporate latitude. What we urgently require is another co-ordinate – corporate longitude. At present, we simply don't systematize the information we have to evaluate these issues. Relying on corporate latitude alone, we are lost in the fog at sea.

COMPASS LINKS
www.disney.com
www.stern.edu
www.baruch-lev.com

TAKING BEARINGS
- How often do you use your annual report to help you make a decision?
- Can you put a value on your company's intangible assets?
- When were your financial reporting systems last changed?

NEW PERSPECTIVES

Luca Pacioli was a true Renaissance man. He was a mathematician, philosopher and more. What we need now are Renaissance perspectives, which take in the full 360 degrees of the compass (as well as the 3D of a gyrocompass) rather than a select portion. Accounting, Pacioli-style, is historical.

To move from Pacioli to the modern world, Andrew Mayo suggests that we need to move:

- from tangible asset management to intangible asset management as well
- from departmental focus to a process and customer focus
- from past orientation to a past and future orientation
- from cost measurement to cost and value measurement
- from work being measured as salary costs to work being measured as percentage of value added
- from cash flow orientation to an orientation on cash flow and future revenue streams
- from indirect cost allocation to departments to indirect cost allocation to value streams
- from fixed budget periods to dynamic budgeting
- from financial data as outcomes to financial data as outcomes and inputs
- from regular period statements to continuing access to company data.

"Numbers of course are here to stay, and for a business financial outcomes will always remain the key measures of success," says Mayo. "The challenges are twofold – to understand transaction management and valuation; and to understand the driving causes of results as well as the results themselves. Accounting is not the same as valuation; it deals in transactions and that is one reason why costs dominate value."[16]

Knowledge economics demands that we develop perspectives on the past, present and the future. As the Disney and Skandia examples show, the past can be a potent competitive advantage. In their approach to the new economy people are sometimes too quick to dismiss what has gone before. Worse, they are unaware of the perspective that history affords. The past should not be ignored.

At the Skandia Future Center people are surprised by the presence of antiques. They think of a Future Center as somewhere clean, air conditioned, disinfected and full of buzzing high-tech equipment. But walking around there you see very few computers and a lot of antiques.

There are old and new things deliberately to offer three time perspectives – the past, the present and the future. We have an antique wooden filing container. This used to be wheeled around offices, for knowledge sharing, so they could put files into it. Very Dickensian, you might think. But we still talk of files in our computers. The language remains the same, as does the basic function.

The past can be a potent competitive advantage. The principle of knowledge management is much the same. So, having the trolleys of 100 years ago helps give a perspective on today's mobile internet. Similarly, we also have a 70-year-old typewriter. We don't use typewriters like that any more but we are still finding it difficult, if not impossible, to agree on where to put the @ symbol on the world's keyboards. Think about it and the issues concerning standards are often much the same; it is just that our times are different. Leonardo recorded his ideas in a notebook. Now we have palmtops. The Center is putting things in context, providing comparisons and benchmark learnings.

We are helping people to get a perspective on the evolving future. As Gary Hamel says, "The perspective is worth 50 IQ points." We want to enable people to see the different opportunities, so they can then put their talent into immediate action. Leonardo said you need at least three perspectives for a good experiment – and you have to be looking in order to find them.

Perspective is a real thing – yet another real thing you won't find on a balance sheet.

First we need a perspective on the present. We need sharper sensitivity to things happening outside otherwise we end up missing major developments and innovations. But the present should not blind us to change, either.

Across the water from the Skandia Future Center is a fortress built by the Swedes in the archipelago to defend the approach to Stockholm. The fortress took 50 years to build. A massive undertaking – especially when you consider that the perceived need for the fortress was based on the scenario that attack was only likely with the weapons which then existed. But as the fortress was being built, the technology of guns changed so that regardless of the size of its walls it was worthless. The Swedes were too busy building to gain a perspective. They built for the present rather than the future. The fortress was later used as a prison. Those who are prisoners to one major perspective or thought model should take note.

What we have to do is get a perspective on the evolving future, see the different opportunities and then put our brain potential into immediate action – internally as well as externally. I am not saying this is easy, but it is necessary.

Traditionally we have been very poor at seeing the present evolving with any degree of accuracy. In the mid-1950s, Peter Drucker predicted there would be 10 to 12 million college students in the US in 20 years' time. This was not guesswork. He simply combined two facts: increased birth rates and rising percentages of young people entering college. Universities rejected Drucker's forecasts and only a few prepared for massively increased numbers. There are countless other similar cases. We have to refine what we see, think and feel now and transform it into actions to shape the future. What I say is that the future is 14 seconds down the road. Grasp it now.

Second, we need a perspective on the past. For managers the past is another country, one they tend to choose to by-pass or dismiss in their mind travels.

But the past cannot be forgotten or dismissed. That's what Mao attempted in the Cultural Revolution and what the management fad of re-engineering was all about. There's a proverb which runs something like "We can't know where we are going if we don't know where we have been" and I think that largely holds true. At Disney, Michael Eisner recognized that the company's heritage presented opportunities. The past was repackaged to revitalize the present. (Jan R. Carendi and Björn Wolrath did much the same at Skandia.)

And then there is the third perspective: the future. People expect the future to be futuristic but learning is about perspective. As the Impressionists said, you have to step back to get the larger pattern. (Or, as modern chaos theory has it, you must step back to see the big from the little.)

We must futurize. While financial accounting is historical, intellectual capital reporting has to be forward looking. For shareholders **The future is 14 seconds down the road.** this is the most important information, as the rest is history or past performance. What has already happened may not be the best guide to the future. We must re-cast the future as an asset otherwise it quickly becomes a liability, an opportunity cost.

In the quest to gain new perspectives, managers have tried various tools and techniques, which offer broader measurements of performance and potential. This suggests they realize there is a problem. A profusion of new tools are launched every year – Andrew Mayo has recently developed the Human Capital Monitor, there is also a "human capital wheel," "human capital index" and Pricewaterhouse-Coopers offers what it labels "HR analytics."[17] Karl-Erik Sveiby proposes his "intangible assets monitor" in his book *The New Organizational Wealth*. In his book *Weightless Wealth*, Dan Andriessen of KPMG Holland proposes the "value explorer." The ICAB suggests "IC rating," Baruch Lev has the "Knowledge Capital Index" and Göran Roos proposes the "IC Index."

One of the best known is the Balanced Scorecard launched in the early 1990s. The Balanced Scorecard is a measurement system that balances financial value and non-financial value. A Balanced Scorecard is typically divided into a number, usually between three and six, of focus areas that have been identified as critical for the company. The focus areas are populated with indicators that are measured.

The Balanced Scorecard recognizes that companies have a tendency to fixate on a few measurements, which blinker their assessment of how the business is performing overall. The Balanced Scorecard focuses management attention on a range of key performance indicators, to provide a balanced view.

It emerged out of the work in the 1980s of Robert Kaplan and Thomas Johnson encapsulated in *Relevance Lost: The rise and fall of management accounting*. Johnson and Kaplan, professors of management accounting, argued that "understanding the reasons behind the obsolescence of existing systems should provide improved rationale for organizational change." Johnson and Kaplan contended that traditional accounting systems reported inaccurate product costs and misleading targets for productivity and efficiency.[18]

Kaplan went on to develop the Balanced Scorecard concept with David Norton. The Scorecard compared running a company to flying a plane. The pilot who relies on a single dial is unlikely to be safe. Pilots must utilize all the information contained in their cockpit. "The complexity of managing an organization today requires that managers be able to view performance in several areas simultaneously," said Kaplan and Norton. "Moreover, by forcing senior managers to consider all the important operational measures together, the balanced scorecard can let them see whether improvement in one area may be achieved at the expense of another."

Balance is clearly preferable to imbalance.

In many ways, it is common sense. Balance is clearly preferable to imbalance.

The Balanced Scorecard is useful in that it takes the over-riding, holistic, emphasis of performance away from strictly financial criteria. It does not, however, provide an explicit enough emphasis on the human focus, which increasingly lie at the heart of sustainability.

A tool more along these lines comes from the tool developed at Skandia (the Skandia Navigator). More of that in a minute. Another contributor to the measuring comes from the management consultancy 2GC Active Management. It has developed a measurement regime for intangible assets, which adheres to widely understood principles but directly involves the people on whom the future success of the company depends. 2GC director, Michael Shulver, says: "Forging links between strategy and management behavior is considered relatively easy in areas such as finance and operations, with a plethora of measurements and targets on offer. Translating these to the 'fuzzy' domains of Intellectual Capital and Knowledge has proved difficult for some organizations."

The 2GC process is based on an enhanced version of the Balanced Scorecard, which expresses an organization's strategy as a set of measurable goals from various stakeholders' perspectives. In creating a "reference" design of Balanced Scorecard in one multi-national firm, 2GC found that, of 33 bases of measurement selected, only four were financial. The rest were all i-capital measurements.[19]

The quest for robust new ways of measuring and understanding corporate performance is encouraging. Those that work best will embrace a multitude of perspectives.

COMPASS LINKS
www.sveiby.com
www.ics.com
www.weightlesswealth.com
www.2GC.co.uk
www.balancedscorecard.org

TAKING BEARINGS
- Does the emphasis in what you measure lie in the past, present or future?
- How do you visualize in numbers your perspectives on the future?
- In what way are these numbers communicated internally and externally?

NAVIGATING THE FUTURE

If you take a balance sheet you can see the traditional assets and debits at the top as book values. Under the surface you see the hidden values. Hidden value is not shown in the balance sheet, but still contributes to the organization's value creation. It is the value tentatively included in market capitalization but inherent in the company's intellectual assets. Usually it is described as goodwill, technology, competencies etc.

When we looked at Skandia in the early 1990s we found more than 50 different items that could be labeled as hidden values. There were, among others, the trademark, the concessions, the customer databases, the IT systems. The list was too long. So we looked for a way to simplify it and a tool to enable us to understand their impact on the business in the past, present and future.

The result was the development of an IC value scheme and the Skandia Navigator in 1992. This emerged in parallel to the work on the Balanced Scorecard – we refined the process dimension of this and put in an emphasis on the human capital of the hidden values. This led to the development of the very first annual report on intellectual capital published internally in 1994 and externally in 1995. This was then followed by public documents and six supplements to the annual report published every six months as prototypes.

The Navigator consists of five value-creating fields. Each focuses on a certain sphere of interest. These are: financial focus; customer focus; process focus; human focus; renewal and development focus and the environmental context.

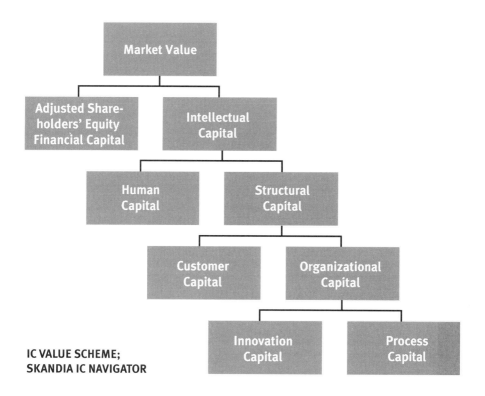

**IC VALUE SCHEME;
SKANDIA IC NAVIGATOR**

Imagine intellectual capital as a building where financial focus is the roof, the uppermost triangle. This is the attic where the recorded accounts are stored – they are history, quietly gathering dust.

External customer relations and internal processes serve as the supporting walls of the building. The foundation and basement of the building is the focus on renewal and development. At the center of the building is, of course, the focus on humans and brain potential.

In the Navigator, the financial focus is our stored past, our achievements so far. The historical perspective. The company's people, customers and processes are its current existence. They are the day-to-day embodiment of the organization. The renewal and development powers form the foundation, the future perspective. Renewal and development are the new bottom line.

Alternatively, it can be useful to compare intellectual capital to a tree. The ripe fruit of the season's efforts can be seen in the crown – the annual report's income statement and balance sheet. The human core in the trunk is protected by the bark of customer relations and work routines. Research and planning, which the tree needs in order to survive future droughts or cold spells, is carried out in the root system in its interaction with the cultivating soil. At a time marked by quick and capricious changes in the business environment, it is in the space of the roots where the most crucial activity may take place for future fruition.

Contrary to traditional accounting, intellectual capital as manifested in the Navigator provides a 3D compass for charting a course towards tomorrow as well as a map of yesterday. The Navigator is a versatile strategic leadership tool for planning, management and follow-up. Moreover, it can be used as a diagnostic tool to trace overheating, fatigue, health, stress or illness in the corporate body (and individual bodies as well).

What the Navigator helps us understand is that intellectual capital is not only a way of assessing intangible assets. It is an active process of value generation. A course of action rather than a store of knowledge. A flow.

The time dimension that's implicit in the Navigator opens the enterprise to a dynamic, more organic view. It nurtures a more rounded perspective.

Traditional accounting presented an anti-holistic view. Look at how it treated profit. Profit is generally seen as the decisive measure of success – by politicians and tax authorities as well as trade unions and company directors. Yet everyone knows how easy it is to manipulate profit. It can be inflated with lofty mortgages in an anticipated future, or be reduced by taking deliberate losses and write-offs. Highlighting the driving forces behind profit creates a more forward-looking leadership perspective.

Basically, the classical balance sheet is a sophisticated abacus. Intellectual capital and the Navigator work more like a melody, smooth rhythmic music. To hear and experience the melody, one must simultaneously think backwards and forwards – entwine the present with the past and the future, with external and internal relations.

The Navigator is not cast in stone. It is not the solution. Its focuses are simply a way of visualizing how various kinds of capital occupy separate spheres of influence. You could easily add other distinct areas. A recent interesting effort comes from Mark McElroy of the Knowledge Management Consortium International (KMCI) who includes Social Innovation Capital in his approach to understanding IC.

Everyone knows how easy it is to manipulate profit.

"When it comes to human beings, the measurement challenge is enormous – people are individuals, they vary with time, and are mobile," writes Andrew Mayo in his book *The Human Value of the Enterprise*. "Choosing measures is one thing, but the process of measurement must have integrity. We believe everything can be quantified, but some areas relating to human capital will be based on perceptions or how well a template fits reality. In these cases the relative movement over time will be more important that an absolute measure."[20]

The optimal solution to all this is reports in real time which give real support to managers. I don't mean instant updates on financial performance – though that is important – but an idea of how indicators are interacting. You might, for example, look at a reading on total revenue in transactions per hour and be able to relate that to employee reward systems.

Successfully implementing intellectual capital and the Navigator requires an extensive IT infrastructure. That used by Skandia –

Dolphin – contains Navigators for each of the company's business units as well as thousands of individuals. Within each there is a wealth of information - facts about employees and partners, competitor profiles, simulation models and much more. Since the systems are all digital, large amounts of data can be presented as numerical overviews in next to real time.

Based on Oracle and Hyperion systems, it also works as a personal knowledge upgrading system and creates collective knowledge. It acts in its next version as an early warning system linked to the mobile phones with Short Message Service to alert people for action.

Of course, no evaluation will ever be perfect. With time and experience, some indicators will be discarded as irrelevant or immeasurable. At the same time, new key ratios will also be discovered.

The choice of indicators is never ending. The aim is clarification not simplification. The more complex, exhaustive and multifaceted the variables and indices are, the better the odds of capturing perspectives of robust benefit to the company's operations and their renewal.

COMPASS LINKS
www.skandia.se
www.intellectualcapital.se
www.kmci.org
www.iccommunity.com

TAKING BEARINGS
- What are the key value drivers of your business?
- How many of them do you measure?
- How are the results of your measurement used to communicate externally especially on renewal and innovation to stakeholders?
- What indicators do you see as informative of value drivers, which would be useful for stakeholders?

Notes

1 "Developing a new economy," *Reform Club*, London 1997

2 "Developing a new economy," *Reform Club*, London 1997

3 Statement of Financial Accounting Concepts, "No. 6, Elements of Financial Statements," FASB, December, 1985

4 Hauser, John, and Katz, Gerald, "Metrics: you are what you measure!," *European Management Journal*, Vol 16 No 5 1998

5 Wallman, Steven and Blair, Margaret, *Unseen Wealth*, Brookings Institute, 2001

6 *Los Angeles Times*, August 1995

7 Beaulieu, Philip; Williams, S Mitchell; & Wright, Michael, *Intellectual capital disclosure practices in Scandinavia*

8 Mayo, Andrew, *The Human Value of Enterprise*, Nicholas Brealey, London, 2001

9 In 2001 the FASB published two reports: "Improving business reporting" and "Business and financial reporting challenges from the new economy."

10 Hall, Robert, "The stock market and capital accumulation," NBER Working Paper 7180, 1999

11 Lev, Baruch, speech at New York University Intangible Capital Conference, May 2001

12 New York University Intangible Capital Conference, May 2001

13 Disney 1999 Annual Report; *Wall Street Journal*, Aug. 3, 2000

14 Sprint 1999 Annual Report; *Wall Street Journal*, Aug. 3, 2000

15 Black, Sandra A, and Lynch, Lisa M., "Human-Capital Investments and Productivity," *American Economic Review*, Vol. 86, No. 2; and Bassi, Laurie J.; Ludwig, Jens; McMurrer, Daniel P.; and Van Buren, Mark, "Profiting from learning: Do firms' investments in education and training pay off?" American Society for Training and Development white paper, Alexandria, VA, September, 2000.

16 Mayo, Andrew, *The Human Value of the Enterprise*, Nicholas Brealey, London, 2001

17 Mayo, Andrew, *The Human Value of the Enterprise*, Nicholas Brealey, London, 2001

18 Johnson, H. Thomas, and Kaplan, Robert, *Relevance Lost: The rise and fall of management accounting*, Harvard Business School, Boston, 1987

19 The full paper on the Measurement of Intellectual Capital is available on 2GC's website www.2gc.co.uk

20 Mayo, Andrew, *The Human Value of the Enterprise*, Nicholas Brealey, London, 2001

1+1=11

The new theory of the firm.

WHERE WE MIGHT BE GOING

I was in an office block in downtown San Francisco. High up. Fifty-seven floors and counting. The light was strong. Then the earthquake struck. I don't know if it was real or imagined, but the structure of the building seemed to shake.

Alongside me in the office was Dee W. Hock, a native of North Ogden, Utah, and then the head of the VISA Corporation. Dee is a man who has come far and, I believe, as do many others, that he also knows where we might be going. Says Hock: "We are in an era of institutional failure. Ahead is the possibility of the regeneration of individuality, liberty, community and ethics such as the world has never known – and a harmony with nature, with one another and with the divine intelligence such as the world has ever dreamed."

Back in Ogden in the 1950s, Dee Hock's career in financial services took off. In 1968, he developed the concept of a global system for the electronic exchange of value and a unique and new form of organization for that purpose: a decentralized, non-stock, for-profit membership institution to be owned by financial institutions throughout the world. VISA was born in 1970.

Hock's vision is now a $1.5 trillion enterprise jointly owned by more than 20,000 financial institutions in more than 200 countries and territories.

As well as becoming a business, Hock's vision has also become a lifetime's passion. He left the company in 1984 (though remains CEO emeritus) to cultivate his lifelong interest in the evolution of institutions, management practices and the nature and extent of change. One of the results of this is the Chaordic Alliance, a global institution linking people and organizations in order to develop, disseminate and implement new, more effective and equitable concepts of commercial, political and social organization.

The Chaordic Alliance is committed to creating the conditions for the formation of practical, innovative organizations that blend competition and cooperation to address critical societal issues. As Dee observes: "Management expertise has become the creation and control of constants, uniformity, and efficiency, while the need has become the understanding and coordination of variability, complexity and effectiveness."[1] Dee Hock's view of the world is very similar in many ways to that of Björn Wolrath and Jan Carendi who brought about the transformation at Skandia.

Dee Hock coined the word "chaord" by borrowing the first syllables from the words CHAos and ORDer. He uses the term chaordic to describe any system of organization that exhibits characteristics of both chaos and order, dominated by neither. In his book *Birth of the Chaordic Age*, Dee defines chaordic as: "1. The behavior of any self-governing organism, organization or system which harmoniously blends characteristics of order and chaos; 2. Patterned in a way dominated by neither chaos or order; 3. Characteristic of the fundamental organizing principles of evolution and nature."[2]

So, chaordic organizations are characterized by flexibility, innovation, adaptability and inclusiveness. They are not neat and tidy. Nor are they fixated on long-term goals or hidebound by strategies laid down from above. "In the Chaordic Age, it will be much more important to have a clear sense of purpose and sound principles within which many specific, short-term objectives can be quickly achieved, than a long-range plan with fixed objectives," says Dee Hock. "Such plans often lead to futile attempts to control events in order to make them fit the plan, rather than understanding events so as to advance by all means in the desired direction."[3] But this is reality. If you design a software program with a bug you haven't done your job properly. If you try to create a system in an organization, bugs are a fact of life. Managing them is part of the job.

Leadership tends to be distributed throughout a chaordic organization rather than concentrated in a management class. No single person or group of persons "runs" it in the way we're used to thinking. Participants largely manage their own affairs as they see fit. When collective action needs to be taken the decision-making process may be based on unanimous consent, on a "sense of the meeting," or perhaps on a majority vote. High value leadership skills may differ from place to place within the organization. Every imaginable kind of leadership is needed to run a chaordic organization. It is never a one-person show.

That being said, chaordic organizations often gravitate to the old-fashioned definition of leadership, namely, "going first and navigating the way." The people within a chaordic organization that take a lead worth following are likely to have company.

There are echoes of chaordic alliances in the concept of "adhocracy", a phrase coined by leadership expert Warren Bennis in the 1960s, and popularized by futurist Alvin Toffler and the strategy guru Henry Mintzberg. An adhocracy is the opposite of bureaucracy. It is an organization that disregards the classical principles of management where everyone has a defined role, in favor of a more fluid organization where individuals are free to deploy their talents as required.

In an adhocracy the concept of what is a worthwhile activity is crucial. Once managers see that unofficial activity is useful, they will start to ring fence and support these pockets. But to be effective, pockets of good practice often have to be kept covert at first. Their creators have to act subversively. It is akin to encouraging new crops before they break through the surface of the soil. Nurturing goes on even though you can't see the green shoots. At a corporate level, this explains why it is necessary to have separate arenas for organizational experimentation like the Skandia Future Center.

The reality is mapped out by Paul Strassmann: "What makes a company prosper is not financial capital – which anyone can obtain for a price – but the effectiveness with which knowledge capital is put to use."[4] We need knowledge entrepreneurs to challenge institutional inefficiencies with new enterprising approaches.

COMPASS LINKS
www.pegasuscom.com
www.chaordicalliance.org
www.skandiafuturecenter.com
www.futurecenter.dk
www.futurecenter.no

TAKING BEARINGS
- Where and how is chaorder evident in your organization?
- Who is in charge of chaos in your organization?
- How do your leaders encourage and reward subversion?
- How do you become a cultivator of chaordic experiments?

WHERE WE ARE

In the past companies were pleased if they could make $1+1=2$. In the knowledge economy, the whole can be many times greater than the sum of the parts. Potentially, $1+1=11$. Research by Paul Romer at Stanford and others suggests that this can be achieved through the multiplier effect of knowledge recipes, combinations, leading to an exponential relationship instead of a linear relationship. "The Knowledge Economy can be a multiplicative economy where we can multiply the significance and value of one another's ideas, inspirations and insight," says Charles Savage of Knowledge Era Enterprises.

Let's retrace our steps a little back along the IC journey. In the evolution of intellectual capital there have so far been four distinct phases:

Phase one focused on the visualization of intangibles from a reporting perspective. This is seen in the supplementary accounting prototyped at Skandia, and now being called for by some organizations, including the Securities and Exchange Commission (SEC) and Financial Accounting Standard Board (FASB) in the US and the Danish government. Special methodologies for this have been developed – they include the Dolphin accounting system at Skandia, an i-capital rating developed by Intellectual Capital Sweden and another now emerging from a new company called IC Growth.

Phase two concerned human capital injection, often labeled competence adding or knowledge management. This is concerned with the aspirations and potential of the new knowledge nomads. It is both the search for talents to be added – by mergers between companies, for example – and the effectiveness from knowledge management and the installation of IT-based knowledge systems.

The third phase is the systematic transformation of human capital into structural capital as a multiplier, with much more sustainable earnings potential for the organization. It is a refined approach based on the second phase, but focused on the packaging of knowledge into multiplicative recipes to be shared globally and rapidly – such as the emerging knowledge exchanges such as *www.knexa.com*. This shifts the focus of leadership from human capital to structural capital as a multiplier of human talents. This was one of the critical strategies of Skandia in exporting its knowledge systems for localized applications. It is the shift to collectively growing structural capital, often simplified to knowledge sharing. (Knowledge sharing is so important that it is one of only three business processes – along with resource and people allocation – for which GE chief Jack Welch was happy to take responsibility.) These knowledge recipes are set to become the new global export items rather than the flow of goods.

The fourth phase is structural capital injection from an external source. This has a turbo effect on the maximizing of IC. It combines different types of structural capital constellations for the joint creation of new opportunities. It is focused on the enterprising space of co-creation, the unique space of imagination and organizational stretch where human capital and structural capital meet. This phase is a matter of sharing and renting each other's invisible structural capital.

Knowledge recipes are set to become the new global export items.

As Kevin Kelly points out, the marginal cost of these new combinations is typically zero, while the upside is huge revenue potential. One illustration of this is the merger between AOL and Time Warner, which combines different organizational capital components with complementary customer capital potential. There is a shift of perspective from a local and physical focus to a global and intangible focus that will shape innovative prime movers. There is also the new, more intangible intellectual entrepreneurship, such as now evident in the TIME (telecom, informatics, media and entertainment) sector.

The possibilities are exciting, but to enjoy the benefits companies need to grasp some fundamentals.

Intangibles have two major components: human capital and structural capital.

Human capital is critical to the innovative success of any company but one that walks out the door every evening. It cannot be owned.

It is the accumulated value of investments in employee training, competence and the future. The term focuses on the value of what the individual can produce; human capital thus encompasses individual value in an economic sense. It can be described as the employees' competence, relationship ability and values. Work on human capital often focuses on transforming individual into collective competence and more enduring organizational capital.

Structural capital is what's left in the company after the people go home – it can be owned.

The mistake has been to see human capital in a vacuum. Human capital requires infrastructure to create a springboard for people's talent potential. This is easier to see in the context of the professions. Take the simple example of a lawyer, an accountant, or a doctor – all hardened knowledge workers. These professionals own their unique abilities to interpret rules and make judgements. Yet none carries an encyclopaedic knowledge of their field in their heads. In the course of their work, they refer to structural capital contained in books – or, by now perhaps, CD ROMs and websites. They need the structural capital. It forms the bedrock of their knowledge. Without it they would be forced to remember everything they had ever learned, and to constantly update their knowledge as rules changed.

When you consult a lawyer, you want his or her interpretation, knowledge and skill in applying that knowledge. Applied knowledge is what you pay all that money for. You'd worry if he or she didn't know where to go to refresh or update that knowledge. Nor would you be happy to simply be handed a law book. Human capital can only flourish if the structure is established to enable it to do so. Either in a void is worthless. Similarly, these knowledge professionals rely on their organizations – the law firm, the accountancy practice, or the hospital – for structural capital.

The multiplier effect of human potential with structural capital (especially with its sub-component organizational capital) is the critical perspective. It can be simplified into an equation:

$$\text{HUMAN CAPITAL} \times \text{STRUCTURAL CAPITAL} = \text{INTELLECTUAL CAPITAL}$$

The point about structural capital is that it can work 24 hours a day. For example, you can obtain medical information from the Internet. This is an area of enormous potential for health services. The virtual knowledge of a leading doctor in the field comes to you. The doctor's knowledge is captured as structural capital that is available when he or she is not. But this doesn't remove the need for the doctor – still less the surgeon.

These ideas are easy to grasp in the context of the professions. But when it comes to other types of knowledge workers the ground appears less firm. In particular, most companies struggle with the notion of organizational capital.

Organizational capital forms a significant part of structural capital. It is the structure of the organization that allows knowledge workers to leverage their talents. Think of the firm as a network. There are other people who belong to the network whose contribution, when combined with fellow knowledge workers, creates value. The surgeon needs the rest of the team – technicians, anaesthetist, nurses. Together they are a team – but a team that is constantly and dynamically changing. The question then becomes, what is the optimal temporary way to organize the human capital at a firm's disposal both inside and outside? How do you create structures which maximize human potential?

Often institutions fail to do so. The human capital moves on and leaves a vacuum. Just look at the transfer of sports players. A star player leaves and a team disintegrates.

Indeed, managers should wonder what they will leave behind when they move jobs? Do any of us really think about the legacy we leave for those who follow? The answer, if you happen to be the chief executive, should be a resounding yes. Any CEO who doesn't think about this critical issue isn't doing the job properly. If you are going to leave nothing behind – no structural capital, no carefully nourished human capital, your achievement is worthless.

It is the structure of the organization that allows knowledge workers to leverage their talents.

"You can walk around any country graveyard to remind yourself that you will be under grass eventually," Peter Job, CEO of Reuters, observed. "It's sensible, therefore, to say how do I want my company to go on after me?" Or, as Gary Hamel puts it, "Do you live off the legacy or do you shape it?"

The notion of organization legacy extends beyond the here and now.

In *The Living Company*, Arie de Geus writes about the managers of long-lived companies: "They succeeded through the generational flow of members, and considered themselves stewards of the long-standing enterprise. Each management generation was only a link in a long chain."

Stewardship is an idea that is increasingly relevant to business. Senior management is the custodian of the values that underpin the culture, conserving them on behalf and for the benefit of the company in the future. This is particularly critical when the founder or founders of a company hand over control. What marks out the great firms from the rest is their ability to create sustainable value. They continuously experience the multiplier effect of innovatively combining human talent with structural capital.

And yet, experience is one of the great mysteries of organizational life. It is assumed that managers benefit from experience. More experience enables better decisions (though only if you learn from experience). But while personal experience is recognized as important, collective corporate experience tends to be overlooked. Corporate memory is the organization's ability to transform and add experiences to the structural capital. The ability to recall, remembering what it is needed when it is needed; animated memory that supports the business processes without stifling innovation.

Art Kleiner, author of *The Age of Heretics*, and George Roth, an MIT researcher, argue that "managers have few tools with which to capture institutional experience, disseminate its lessons and translate them into effective action."[5] To do so, they suggest using a tool called the learning history – "a narrative of a company's recent set of critical episodes, a corporate change event, a new initiative, a widespread innovation, a successful product launch or even a traumatic event like a downsizing." The histories can be anything from 25 to 100 pages in length and are arranged in two columns. In one column the people involved in the events describe what happened. In the opposite column are comments and observations from grandly titled "learning historians." These are consultants and academics from outside the organization though people from inside the corporation may also comment. The commentary draws out the lessons, trends and conclusions, which can be drawn from the narrative. The history can then be dialogued by groups.

Kleiner and Roth believe all this is related to ancient community story telling. The method, they say, builds trust. People are asked about their version of events. They can speak out without fear on subjects which may have concerned them for years – the

> **What marks out the great firms is their ability to create sustainable value.**

contributions are anonymous. Most importantly, learning histories can allow an organization to transfer experience from one division to another. The end result could be organizations which genuinely learn from experience and "a body of generalizable knowledge about management." (A similar approach around storytelling, taken by Stephen Denning, has proven to be very successful at the World Bank.[6])

What we leave behind is structure, codified learnings and explicit knowledge. Our legacy and the organizational capital must be built around a structure, which aims to make knowledge explicit.[7]

Peter Drucker argues that the great management achievement of the last century was to increase the productivity of manual workers 50-fold. While this cannot be under-estimated, it is not the great challenge of the new century. This, according to Drucker, is to increase the productivity of knowledge workers – dauntingly he estimates that the productivity of some knowledge workers has actually declined over the last 70 years.

This is the nub of the problem. We have not developed effective organizational structures to optimize the efforts of knowledge workers. What we have at present are two extremes. Traditional companies have industrial organizational structures, which struggle to cope with the volatility of the knowledge economy. Some new economy companies, meanwhile, have taken away the old structure without putting anything sustainable in its place. As jazz musician Miles Davis observed, "You got to improvise on something." And, in the organizational world, that "something" is intangible assets.

Individuals will have a bigger say in how their talents are used.

As yet, most companies still prefer to bury their heads in the sand. The challenge in the next few years will be to address this issue. Once again, we need to shake off our old perspectives and see anew. "Structure is something you create to help you do business more effectively and successfully," says Jonas Ridderstråle, co-author of *Funky Business*. "The challenge now is to build an organizational form capable of simultaneously acting as a bureaucracy, meritocracy and adhocracy. While it is true that the traditional bureaucracy has had a bad press if its best elements are not acknowledged the result is usually anarchy. We need to take the best of every organizational model and make it work for us."

What is clear is that the new structures will be looser, less firm, more free flowing and more chaordic. Individuals will have a bigger say in how their talents are used. But this does not mean that we will all be free agents. Far from it. Some might work in global networks of organizational capital combined with local human capital and customer capital. The great lesson of the knowledge economy is that new combinations of talent create new value. Continuous and rapid reconfiguration is the name of the game. This speed is called "organizational float" by Dee Hock. Value resides in the new combinations, the springboard effects, we can create – together. 1+1=11.

COMPASS LINKS
www.well.com
www.intellectualcapital.se
www.stevedenning.com

TAKING BEARINGS
- How does your organization nurture its memory?
- How does your organization move from individual IC mode to collective IC mode?
- What is your organizational capability to multiply human and structural capital into intellectual capital?
- What will your legacy be?
- What are the proportions of human capital and structural capital in your organization?

NEW SHAPES AND METAPHORS

"Quite often in knowledge management, organizations have been traditionally seen as entities that could be understood," says David Snowden of IBM's Institute of Knowledge Management. However, in this new age of uncertainty, we need more flexibility and responsiveness than can be readily provided by a mechanical understanding of an organization. We need to be able to sense change on receipt of partial data, to respond in such a way as to reduce uncertainty, and to enable the organization to be agile enough to be in the right place at the right time. These are the survival characteristics of the modern resilient corporation.

"Intellectual capital is too diverse, too complex, and too heavily dependent on individuals and communities who do not behave rationally. Neither do we want them to behave rationally – to do so would drive out innovation and relationships, both of which are skills for the knowledge economy."[8]

As David Snowden suggests, to exploit human capital, to exploit structural capital, the organization of the future will be different, profoundly so. If 1+1 is equal to 11, the way we think about the firm must change. The way we shape organizations must change. The way we talk about organizations and the way we imagine organizations must change. This is the quest for intelligent enterprising.

First let's look at shape.

"Years from now, we won't define a big corporation in terms of the number of people who work for it," notes Robert Reich.[9] "The so-called big corporation of the future will be a big brand. It will have a big capacity to generate trust among consumers and give them the quality they want. Arrayed around these big brands will be large numbers of small teams. Some of them will be independent companies. Some of them, while part of the big corporation, will be independent profit centers. Some will be units that are quasi-independent. Some will be project teams that move from project to project. The real creative work will be done in groups ranging in size from 15 to 100."

> **If 1+1 is equal to 11, the way we think about the firm must change.**

Bob Johansen of the Institute for the Future envisages what he calls the "fishnet organization" made up of individuals organized in small, temporary, cross-organizational, time-focused, task-driven groups, usually called teams.

Whatever organizational shape we imagine, some sort of structured organization is always needed. The "virtual organization" model has struggled to be accepted precisely because of the lack of structure it offers. As a result, the world's best minds are now wrestling with a host of potential organizational models which attempt to make sense of the world around and how people now work and think.

The Canadian guru Don Tapscott, for example, talks of the arrival of "a new business form" which is made up of "fluid congregations of businesses – sometimes highly structured, sometimes amorphous – that come together on the Internet to create value for customers and wealth for their shareholders." This new organizational form is labelled by Tapscott a "business web" or "b-web."

Business webs are a "universal business platform" made up of "a distinct system of suppliers, distributors, commerce services providers, infrastructure providers and customers."

Along similar lines is the notion of the "networked incubator." "The distinguishing feature of a networked incubator is that it has mechanisms to foster partnerships among start-up teams and other successful Internet-oriented firms, thus facilitating the flow of knowledge and talent across companies and the forging of marketing and technology relationships between them," conclude Harvard Business School's Morten T. Hansen, Henry W. Chesbrough, Nitin Nohria and Donald N. Sull in a study of the incubator market.

In some ways this is way too formalized. Flexibility and looseness are the characteristics of networks that work. I prefer Brian Arthur's idea of "loose alliances" – "Unlike products of the processing world, such a soybeans and rolled steel, technological products exist within local groupings of products that support and enhance them. They exist in mini-ecologies. This interdependence has deep implications for strategy. In fact, if technological ecologies are now the basic unit of strategy in the knowledge-based world, players compete not by locking in a product on their own but by building webs – loose alliances of companies organized around a mini-ecology – that amplify positive feedback to the base technology," writes Arthur.[10]

The new organizational models also include cafés and circuses. After all, where does the exchange of ideas work best? The kitchen or the boardroom? The relaxed atmosphere of the kitchen – or any other such space – is more conducive to the kind of thinking and behavior required of modern managers and organizations. At Skandia, this was prototyped at the Skandia Future Center and then applied in various places. For example, Skandia's office in Vienna included a Viennese-style café to encourage cultural bonding between employees from various nationalities.

The knowledge café concept has been explored by Juanita Brown.[11] In 1994, Juanita and I hosted the opening of a pioneering knowledge dialogue on intellectual capital at her home in California's Mill Valley. The meeting was arranged like a Viennese café with various conversations going on around tables in the house. The result was the creation of a powerful series of dialogues. "Intuitively I knew that we had accidentally tapped into something very basic, something that felt familiar but that I had never actually experienced in this way," Juanita recalls. "Something very simple, but potentially very powerful. It was almost as if the intelligence of a larger self had made itself visible to us through the café conversations. The knowledge café process had somehow enabled us to become more aware not only of our individual knowledge but also of our collective knowledge at increasing levels of scale."

Juanita has moved the concept on. Groups of up to 1000 have been involved in "café learning conversations." The issues they have covered range from fostering treaty negotiations with Maori leaders in New Zealand to scenario planning in Mexico. Now a variety of developments have been made to the initial idea – these range from Passion Café to Story Café and Friday Café. All take the format and atmosphere of a café to foster and nurture discussion.

Where does the exchange of ideas work best? The kitchen or the boardroom?

Similarly, circuses – a travelling troupe of highly skilled entertainers – are a more illustrative model for the modern organization than those traditionally held dear by theorists and practitioners alike.

Far fetched? Perhaps, though the logic of the circus model may not be as extreme or unreal as you might think. The invention company ?What If!'s annual innovation forum is part circus, part conference. Fire eaters, magicians, stilt walkers, and snake handlers help free delegates from their corporate mindsets and make them more receptive to a cast of speakers specially selected for their provocative messages. "It's all about ways to run a business in a way that encourages innovation," says Adrian Simpson, one of the event's organizers. "In a lifeless, soul-less workplace, what chance do people have of coming up with new ideas?"

According to Simpson, innovation techniques that work share four common characteristics: "Bravery – getting used to putting your head above the parapet; passion – understanding that a belief and a love of what you do moves mountains; freshness – making an effort to organize new sources of stimulation and provocation to help view your organization in different ways; and action – getting on with what you can practically do, as ideas are ultimately useless, unless they see the commercial light of day." Walking along a high wire or putting your head in a lion's mouth is certainly likely to increase the executive's freshness and bravery.

Too extreme? Perhaps, but history and reality suggest that most organizations will emerge as unique hybrids of new and old. Militaristic despots will exercise control in rooms that have been tested for feng shui. Companies will be built around cafés but, while the latte flows, intricate reporting mechanisms will emerge. Bureaucracy will live alongside café society.

As new organizational shapes and structures are being explored so, too, is a new language. New organizations require new metaphors and new stories. New bearings require a new language, a rich vocabulary of new metaphors and images. The old language of business is a barrier to new ways of thinking. We need a new taxonomy.

In their 1995 book *The Knowledge Creating Company*, Ikujiro Nonaka and Hirotaka Takeuchi explained the role of metaphors: "A metaphor or an analogy is a distinctive method of perception. It is a way for individuals grounded in different contexts and with different experiences to understand something intuitively through the use of imagination and symbols. No analysis or generalization is needed. Through metaphors, people put together what they know in new ways and begin to express what they know but cannot yet say. As such, metaphor is highly effective in fostering direct commitment to the creative process in the early stage of knowledge creation."[12]

The old language of business is a barrier to new ways of thinking.

Think of the term "horsepower" which, even now, we use to describe the power of an internal combustion engine. Yet it was only developed to provide a metaphor, a benchmark. People understood how powerful horses were. Actually, watts would have been a more precise measure. What we are interested in is the energy generated. Today, it is the economic energy and vitality of organizations that we should be interested in.

Language evolves. This is even more clear when you consider that throughout the twentieth century the dominant metaphor of working life was that of a machine. Corporations were machines – gigantic engines of capitalism. In a world based on physical capital and industrial power, the successful corporation mirrored the world around it. It was a robot of an organization – a tank that could roll over smaller rivals. It churned out physical products with admirable efficiency. This, people thought, made perfect sense. Survival of the fittest meant survival of the biggest.

Or, take the word "firm." In the business context, a firm is the name or title under which a company conducts business. But it also means securely or solidly fixed, as in terra firma; a prison for talent. Now, knowledge intensive companies need dynamic metaphors for flows and relationships with imagination rather than metaphors, which are static and fixed.

It might be more relevant to visualize the new economical sphere from a biological perspective, as a nervous system with energy flows and cells being split, mutated and evolving. It describes life, renewal and movement. The random and bewildering changes experienced by bacteria are more akin to the rapidly changing shapes required of today's organizations.[13]

Throughout the twentieth century the dominant metaphor of working life was that of a machine.

Consequently, it also highlights institutional failures. According to one report, 45 percent of corporate failure is related to strategic neglect; 38 percent is related to organizational ineffectiveness; and only 17 percent is related to exogenous factors. In other words, where there is a lack of organizational renewal, there is bad organizational float.

Another metaphor I have used is that of the weather forecast and topographic landscape.[14] This uses tools, which are now becoming available that allow users to visually explore multivariate data in a variety of methods. This 3D-diagrammatic reasoning extracts knowledge from company data by converting and crystallizing it into an interactive, forecasting, three-dimensional landscape (see figure below). This can be applied to intellectual capital. It maps a powerful ingest of observation data from databases, applications, operating systems, and hardware platforms linked together into a value shaping model.

Using this IC map, users can interactively query the landscape, perform what-if analysis, and navigate the IC journey in their organization.

The search for alternative metaphors is not new. There have been voices at the fringes for many years. In his 1933 book, *The Human Problems of an Industrial Civilization*, Elton Mayo proposed new images. As a biologist, he regarded corporations as organic systems,

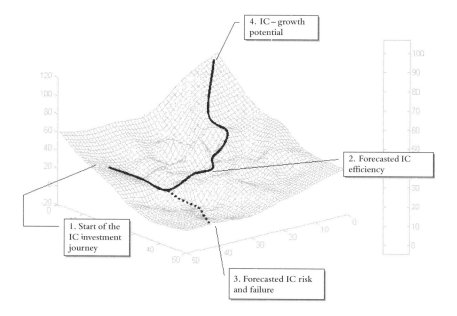

1. Start of the IC investment journey

2. Forecasted IC efficiency

3. Forecasted IC risk and failure

4. IC – growth potential

Where you're going, and what's around you?

Transparency of hidden IC-parameters may be achieved (in time series) by a new ("qlikable") mapping technology. The vertical scale to the left shows – in million $ – the (IAS auditable) IC-growth potential (Source: Accounting code 9230). The mathematical functions underlying the "downscaled" x- and y-axes generate the pattern that makes the organization's past trajectory, and its current heading visual, communicable and easier understandable.

complex and perpetually altering beings. "Living organism is best conceived as a number of variables in equilibrium with each other in such a fashion that a change in any one will introduce changes throughout the whole organization," wrote Mayo.[15]

Mayo was ahead of his time. "We need to think less like managers and more like biologists," advises the contemporary thinker, MIT's Peter Senge. "The most universal challenge that we face is the transition from seeing our human institutions as machines to seeing them as embodiments of nature." Senge suggests that our faith in the concept of the company as machine has hindered the development of the network of inter-personal relationships, which make up enterprising.[16]

Senge has taken a new look at what we mean by structure. He now defines structure as "a pattern of interdependency that we enact." Interdependency makes redundant the notion of the heroic leader. True, long-lasting, powerful change is not led by an isolated leader, but evolves from small groups. Senge suggests that the roots of change within organizations are pilot groups – "People don't necessarily want to have a vision at work or to conduct dialogue. They want to be part of a team that's fun to work with and that produces results they are proud of." Irresistibly simple and powerfully put by Senge, though history suggests that leaders will succeed in adding their own complexity.

Overall, the language of business needs to be re-oriented. The most fruitful potential source for inspiration is the fast moving world of science. Listen to the advice of Danah Zohar: "Science has direct implications for management. Science talks about 'complex-adaptive systems' and organizations potentially are complex-adaptive systems (holistic, self-organizing, emergent systems). Management needs new thinking; science provides it. Good science respects no paradigm; it questions all assumptions. Management could do with a good dose of such subversive thinking."[17] Evolution requires entrepreneurial subversion.

COMPASS LINKS
www.mit.edu
www.theworldcafe.com
www.kmagazine.com
www.emerald-library.com
www.worldcafe.dk

TAKING BEARINGS
- What metaphor would visualize your enterprising organization?
- How does your internal and external networking evolve?
- How can you cultivate your learning dialogues by organizing knowledge cafés?
- Where is your organization located in the IC landscape?

CREATING INTELLIGENT ENTERPRISING

New metaphors, new models, new organizations. In the knowledge economy organizations must re-create themselves as intelligent enterprises. Intelligent enterprising is what we must now seek at every organization turn.

The notion of intelligent enterprising develops from those developed by James Brian Quinn and Peter Senge. Quinn's 1992 book, *Intelligent Enterprise*, provided an organizational blueprint for the 1990s. In it, Quinn introduced such organizational shapes as the "starburst," the "spider's web," "inverted" and "infinitely flat." Quinn was among the very first to recognize that knowledge and service-based activities and the leveraging of intellectual assets are key to sustained success.

The work of Peter Senge has been influential in convincing companies that the ability to learn is a key success factor for organizations. Senge has undoubtedly done a great deal to develop the concept of the learning organization.

For the traditional company, the shift to becoming a learning organization poses huge challenges. In the learning organization managers are researchers and designers rather than controllers and overseers. Senge argues that managers should encourage employees to be open to new ideas, communicate frankly with each other, understand thoroughly how their companies operate, form a collective vision and work together to achieve their goal.

These points are absolutely crucial to underpin intelligent enterprising. But the structure of intelligent enterprising is an organism that must evolve to maximize its value potential. My concern is that a learning organization is like an over-mature student staying too long at university. It may be having a good time, but it is focused on learning for learning's sake. Intelligent enterprising is focused on blending skills, knowledge and other intangibles, and then quickly applying them to create new value. It is externally focused.

I echo some of Tom Stewart's comments on the learning organization. "I don't really know what the 'learning organization' is," he said in one interview. "As I've looked at it, it seems to have wandered off into very personal, solipsistic stuff. Like, do I love my boss, does my boss love me; spiritual values; that sort of thing. I won't say those things are not important, but they are an effect not a cause. Every company says 'We need better communication,' so they increase from 20 newsletters and 30 videotapes to 29 newsletters and 55 videotapes. The fact is better communication comes from working together. If you and I are working together, and sharing knowledge, we will in fact communicate. I think the corporate issue is best addressed by focusing on the work, and bringing valuable knowledge to bear on the work, and then the learning will follow; the community, the spirit and all that will follow. I don't think you can address the culture directly. But I see much of the conversation about the 'learning organization' as just flailing around about culture."[18]

Intelligent enterprising differs from a learning organization in two dimensions. First, it is focused on learning and knowledge as a source of value creation. Period. Its output is new combinations of knowledge. Second, its emphasis is on teaching, knowledge sharing and on framing, making sense of the approaching future, rather than sifting the past.

The learning organization is the starting point. Intelligent enterprising is the goal. Intelligent enterprising combines rational intelligence, emotional intelligence and spiritual intelligence. It has the capability to analyze, and socialize knowledge. But it also has the intelligence that make these activities meaningful to its people.

Intelligent enterprising is where the learning organization grows up and joins the real world, where the focus is on distributing the learning process as rapidly as possible to capitalize knowledge potential. The lead-time between learning and teaching might be the best indicator of the organizational float, or IQ, of intelligent enterprising. Knowledge accumulation and exploitation becomes its raison d'être rather than a useful initiative. The onus is on stimulating and sharing. Intelligent enterprising has a number of characteristics:

Linking learning to performance and reward

At Motorola, learning is directly related to individual performance and reward. This is integral to intelligent enterprising.

Learning can be stimulated in a variety of ways. Motorola has something it called the "Individual Dignity Entitlement," a quarterly survey which is linked to the bonuses of its managers. The questions it poses are simple but far-reaching:

- Do you have a substantive meaningful job that contributes to the success of Motorola?
- Do you have on-the-job behaviors and the knowledge base to be successful?
- Has training been identified and been made available to continuously upgrade your skills?

- Do you have a career plan and is it exciting, achievable and being acted on?
- Have you received candid positive or negative feedback within the last 30 days, which has been helpful in improving your performance or achieving your career plan?
- Is there appropriate sensitivity to your personal circumstances, gender and cultural heritage?

Sharing knowledge

Xerox has set about encouraging and enabling knowledge sharing. It has developed, for example, an internet system called Eureka! connected to a database, which allows its repair technicians to share tips about repairs. Eureka! is now put to work by 15,000 Xerox technicians who make over 250,000 repair calls every year. It is estimated to save the company a massive $11 million per year.

Xerox's approach is built around the notion that initiatives are worthless unless knowledge sharing is ingrained as part of the company's culture. Knowledge sharing can become bogged down in technology. "We started with an intense search around workers – what makes them tick, what's important, what problems they are solving – and then picked technology that suits the solutions," says Xerox's Don Holtshouse. Its emphasis is on allowing initiatives the freedom to prosper or fail.[19]

Intelligent enterprising is also concerned with sharing knowledge. "We must think of ourselves less as insurance specialists and more as specialists in collaboration," noted Skandia deputy CEO Jan Carendi.[20]

Or, as John Seely Brown puts it: "The only sustainable competitive edge we have is to be able to learn faster than our competitors and to share what we have learned (knowledge) more effectively than our competitors."[21]

Trust is the bridge for knowledge sharing and knowledge sharing is the difference between individual and collective knowledge. To work, knowledge sharing needs explicit codified taxonomy, a modus operandi. "Organizations have so far concentrated on developing the IT systems needed to capture and manage knowledge," says Christina Evans, author of a report on knowledge management and an associate of the UK's Roffey Park management center. "Now they need to create the environmental conditions and organizational practices which will enable knowledge sharing, as opposed to knowledge hoarding." (This takes us back to the knowledge café as a tool for cultural bonding which nourishes exchange and the sharing of knowledge.)

Collaboration is a matter of external alliances and harvesting internal knowledge. "Knowledge sharing is going to become part of a fabric inside the company for all employees," predicts Xerox's Don Holtshouse.[22] Brave words, but research repeatedly suggests that knowledge sharing does not come easily. The problem is, essentially, that the knowledge which resides within an organization chiefly can be found in the brains of employees. (And Xerox has 90,000 of them.) One executive calculates that "only two percent of information gets written down – the rest is in people's heads." A study of over 700 US companies found that 12 percent of corporate knowledge can be found on electronic knowledge bases; 20 percent in electronic documents; 26 percent in paper documents and 42 percent in the brains of employees.

Creating knowledge sharing structures

Knowledge sharing needs to be more freewheeling than other activities. Bureaucracy and budget-related form filling needs to be kept to a minimum.

If it feels institutional, it probably won't work all that well. PricewaterhouseCoopers has an intranet, which gets 18 million hits a month. Successful, you might think, but perhaps more useful and powerful is an independent network of 500 people which emerged naturally. Called "Kraken," the network is a loose, ill-defined group of people who want to maximize their innovative potential. Anyone within PwC can join. There is no huge technological back-up. It is informal, not institutionalized. It works. Combine the corporate might with the renegade offshoot and you have something very powerful indeed.

Tom Stewart has also highlighted Ford's success in knowledge sharing – though he has also lamented the fact that Ford and Firestone's inability to share knowledge was a contributory factor to the unhappy experience of Firestone tires on Ford Explorers. Even so, Stewart says that Ford's Best Practices Replication Process has yielded a payback to the company of over $1 billion.[23]

The process began life in 1996 and has meant that over 2,800 "superior practices" have been shared across the automaker's manufacturing operations. As an additional bonus, the process has also now been licensed to Royal Dutch/Shell and Nabisco. The Ford Process, Stewart reports, had some simple founding principles: "First, the process would be managed, with distinct roles and responsibilities. Simple organisms don't need central nervous systems; complex ones can't live without them. Second, no practice would get into the system unless proven. Third, every improvement would be described in the language of the work group involved: time, head count, gallons, quality." The result is a step by step process – 42 steps in total – which works. The lessons? "First, knowledge is best shared within communities.

Like a magnet, the task draws knowledge from its hiding places.

People with something in common talk more than strangers do," says Tom Stewart. "Second, the more widely dispersed knowledge is, the more powerful the force required to share it. Such a force supports Ford's Best Practices Replication Process in manufacturing. Every year Ford headquarters hands down a "task" to managers – they're required to come up with a 5 percent, 6 percent, or 7 percent gain in, say, costs, throughput, or energy use. The best-practices database is the first place managers turn to after getting their task. Like a magnet, the task draws knowledge from its hiding places."

The challenge ahead is to move from best practice to being able to select the best option. This is closer to what is done by Buckman Laboratories, a $250 million producer of industrial chemicals headquartered in Memphis, Tennessee. Buckman Laboratories has been a pioneer in knowledge management with K'Netix (The Buckman Knowledge Network). Its efforts have been awarded The Arthur Andersen Enterprise Award in 1996 and the 1997 Computerworld/ Smithsonian Award for innovative applications of technology in the manufacturing category, among many others.

Buckman has benefited greatly from the high-level leadership and inspiration of its chief executive, Bob Buckman. When he took over the firm from his father he encouraged employees to begin looking outward for ideas, searching the globe for new techniques and innovations that might be successfully adopted. Travel expenditures, under his direction, went way up.

"Some of the cultural steps we have taken are designed to get our associates comfortable with this new way of doing business," says Buckman. "For example, we have a global electronic break room for the sharing of trivial stuff that is accessible by everybody. People get comfortable sharing jokes, etc. and then the sharing of important knowledge comes naturally. In addition, we pay for our associates' personal use of the Internet. We want them to be comfortable operating in this new world. By paying these network charges, we also send a message that we trust them to do this intelligently. Play is an important element in the building of communities."[24]

As knowledge is shared it becomes explicit and can be captured.

But Bob Buckman also promoted the development of new information systems that would facilitate the sharing and transfer of knowledge.

"Nobody has a problem using other people's knowledge as long as they don't have to credit the other person with it. There's always that not-invented-here thinking that is a barrier to using knowledge in an organization. When we talk about culture, there are things beyond just encouraging people and giving recognition and promotions. The difficulty with rewards and recognition is that it is sometimes seen as unfair because it is so hard to measure knowledge transfer," says Tim Meek, Buckman's vice-president of knowledge transfer.

Of course, none of this is easy. As Meek explains: "It's work to share knowledge and it takes time that people don't seem to have. When people see top management doing something a certain way, it encourages them to do it themselves. People are boss-watchers. Bob [Buckman] was very visible from the very beginning, driving the movement both by example and by mandate. He would say that he didn't mandate it. But when you get a note from Bob saying that 'I notice you're not in our discussion forum lately. Are you having problems? We're here to help you, and it's important that you do this. Just want to make sure that you're not having any technical problems or that you don't need additional training.' When you get a note like that from Bob, you get the message."

In that vein, the company began strongly encouraging both a knowledge sharing culture and the use of mobile global electronic networks to facilitate continuous knowledge sharing and communication. Buckman Labs' knowledge transfer department – which oversees help desk services, software/hardware support, applications development, network services and a knowledge resources center (which makes marketing, product and technical information available to the entire organization) – has been instrumental in ensuring that the enterprise develops a culture of open exchange.

As knowledge is shared it becomes explicit and can be captured and knowledge that is captured is structural capital that can be a springboard for innovation and value creation.

Balancing chaos and order

Here we encounter a fundamental organizational dichotomy. Formal structure and processes can stifle creativity – but without them ideas are unlikely to be harnessed. Innovation, then, requires an intelligent blending of structure and creativity – back, perhaps, to the word chaordic. Take the example of Xerox again.

From his vantagepoint at Xerox PARC John Seely Brown (now retired) has observed the flow of ideas through the innovation process. In a *Harvard Business Review* article – "How to capture knowledge without killing it" – he and social theorist Paul Duguid discuss the tension between practice and process. The arrival of the Internet, they note, has been a disruptive influence for middle managers. They have been confronted with two radically different visions of what managing in the new economy means.[25]

Initially, companies re-engineered their business processes in the belief that it would improve efficiency and provide sustainable competitive advantage. Corporations spent billions of dollars. But just as the re-engineers breathed a collective sigh of relief, they were told that the process was out of date. The new business imperative was knowledge management. It suggested that businesses that could capture the knowledge embedded in their organizations would own the future.

The problem, say Seely Brown and Duguid, is that re-engineering and knowledge management are "profoundly different approaches. Re-engineering is about the structured co-ordination of people and information. It's top-down. It assumes that organizations compete in a predictable environment. Knowledge management focuses more on effectiveness than on efficiency. It's bottom-up. It assumes that organizations compete in an unpredictable environment."

They suggest that the shift from re-engineering, or process engineering, to knowledge management represents something more significant than just a change of corporate fashion. It throws up a dilemma that all managers have to wrestle with. This is "the organizational tension between process, the way things are formally organized, and practice, the way things actually get done."

This is the dichotomy at the heart of organizations. Move too far towards practice and the organization lacks the infrastructure to

Too much process and you kill creativity altogether.

turn ideas into something useful. Too much process and you kill creativity altogether. The leadership challenge is to have agile organizational capital that combines innovative practice and process effectively on a global scale.

Using Xerox as a case study, Seely Brown and Duguid explain how a judicious balance between the two approaches can create constructive processes, which support innovation. At Xerox, for example, blending practice and process includes regular get-togethers where the service engineers who carry out repairs on Xerox machines can discuss their own best practices. Laid on top of this is a process involving a peer-review system to collect, vet and disseminate the best ideas to the rest of the organization.

This is admirable. It is a good example of a knowledge community. But intelligent enterprising requires that knowledge communities are integrated in such a way that the engineers' knowledge is effectively channeled into R&D. Knowledge communities are like parts of the corporate brain. The part of the brain that knows how to repair copying machines does not inform the design and development of copying machines.

COMPASS LINKS
www.xerox.com
www.buckman.com
www.kmworld.com
www.intelligententerprise.com
www.chaordic.org

TAKING BEARINGS
- What is the lead-time in your organization between learning and sharing knowledge with others?
- How much of organizational time is spent on learning rather than knowledge sharing?
- How do you cultivate and reward knowledge sharing in your organization?

HOLISTIC ENTERPRISING

Intelligent enterprising demands a holistic view. What are needed is the organizational synapses that make the human brain the inter-connected holistic wonder that it is. As with the human brain, the synapses – conduits for the flow of electricity – are created by an experience or learning opportunity. You cannot simply run knowl-edge cables or pipelines between different departments in the organization. They occur naturally. This requires the active commit-ment of people.

Think of human intelligence. Everyone knows about IQ, and many of us now know about EQ, emotional intelligence. The latest research suggests that there is a third form of intelligence – SQ, or spiritual synapse quotient. This is the ability to put our actions, experiences and life discoveries into a bigger and more meaningful context. SQ sits above IQ and EQ, and nourishes them.

The traditional IQ test measures rational intelligence – the skills we use to solve logical or strategic problems. For a long time, IQ results were considered the best measurement of a person's potential for success. But in the early 1990s Daniel Goleman pointed out that success is also dependent on emotional intelligence – EQ – the thinking that gives us empathy, compassion, and the ability to respond appropriately to pain or pleasure.

Most recently, Tony Buzan, Danah Zohar, and Ian Mitchell have claimed that there is another important dimension to intelligence –Spiritual Intelligence, or SQ (synapse quotient). In fact, they assert that SQ is the necessary foundation for both the IQ and the EQ. It is our ultimate intelligence. After all, computers have high IQ, ani-mals often have high EQ, but only humans have SQ – the ability to be creative, change the rules, alter situations, and question why we are here. This is what differentiates intelligent enterprising.

"IQ is our rational, logical, linear intelligence," explains Zohar. "It is the intelligence with which we solve problems and with which we manipulate and control our environment. EQ, our emo-tional intelligence, is the intelligence with which we identify the situation we are in and behave appropriately. EQ is an adaptive intelligence. Both IQ and EQ work within a paradigm, within the box, within the given. We use them to play a 'finite game'.

"SQ, our need for and access to deep meaning, purpose and values, is our transformative intelligence. SQ makes us ask fundamental questions, it rocks the boat and moves the boundaries. SQ allows us to understand situations deeply, to invent new categories of understanding, and to be creative. With SQ we play an 'infinite game'."[26]

The trouble is that the short-term nature of business means that the IQ tends to be utilized more regularly than any other form of intelligence. IQ is technical rather than emotional, physical or spiritual. Unfortunately, intellectual capital and knowledge management have often been imposed at this level rather than at a more innovative or profound level. Says London Business School's Sumantra Ghoshal: "To say knowledge management hasn't delivered the goods is an exaggeration. But overall, organizations haven't reaped the benefits predicted. Many companies initially saw knowledge management as a technical task and handed it over to their IT people, who went away and created sophisticated IT systems. But it's really a social not technological issue. Where it has been effective it is because much more attention was put on the human dimension – the social, emotional and relational context." The social, emotional and relational contexts are now of paramount importance. This is also why arenas for prototyping new organizational contexts are needed.

Professor Ghoshal is also sceptical about creating an internal market for knowledge. Companies, he says, must address human capital at a more profound level. "Often we make the mistake of thinking of human capital as just knowledge. A second important aspect is social capital – networks and relationships. The third dimension is emotional capital – the ability and willingness to act. There is no solution other than a trust-based culture. It's not so much I have this knowledge which I give to you, it's more how do you shape questioning and frame learning. At BP, for example, a quarter of the knowledge management budget is spent on coaching people. If you look at Skandia, what it is trying to do is institutionalise questioning. What is special about the company is not the tools it uses but its attempts to embed curiosity in the culture."

Curiosity is not a short-term phenomenon. But cultures are, too often, built for the short-term and little else. "Business lives for the fast buck, the consequences be damned. Business is very bad at looking inward, at evaluating itself, at asking itself uncomfortable questions. Business works in a short time frame rather than cultivating the long-term perspective. Most business practice undermines any kind of reflective thought, using only its IQ to solve immediate problems," says Danah Zohar. "We need people who can think deeply, independently, and radically. We need reflective people who know how to ask good questions. Some universal training in philosophy would go a long way! All our answers today are leading us towards disaster. We need better questions. We need people who will put service above self, people who have the courage to be spontaneous, and people who aren't afraid to get it wrong. We need people who can live at the edge of chaos, between boring predictability and disruptive innovation, between the known and the unknown."

Perhaps the person who provides the most holistic view of these issues is Tony Buzan. "Undoubtedly, there is growing attention on the brain. It is becoming the world's number one focus of attention," he says. "When you know the power of the brain it is blindingly obvious."

Tony Buzan has built his career and life around a restless curiosity. Listen to the story of how he developed his tool of Mind Mapping:

"At university I increasingly found it difficult to finish big essays. There was so much knowledge. I was interested in everything so I couldn't see why I couldn't study everything. It was like confetti and I wanted to grab it in a way that gave it an organized structure. And then I began to develop mind mapping.

"One of the things I did was to design my own diary, which I still use. At the beginning of the year I plan out the main areas of activity. It is knowledge management. If you're going to manage knowledge the first thing you have to manage is the knowledge manager and that is the brain. If you manage it then it manages itself. It is a self-managing system but needs the correct formula if it is to be managed. It needs the correct software programmes. I work out at the beginning of the year how many times I will lecture and so on. Then I look at the months. Everything's color co-ordinated.

"As well as the diary, I captured the data at university through mind mapping."

As Buzan puts it: "Knowledge is not linear. A book is not linear. All kinds of things radiate from your head when you have an idea.

It is like an explosion, a supernova. It is in 360 degrees, three dimensions. That's what a mind map helps to capture."

Mind Maps are ornate, colourful, sometimes beautiful, captures of human thought, a kind of mental shorthand. Using the technique, one page of paper can become a 100-page report. "If I come back to a mind map in 20 years I will know instantly what it was about. It is the visualization of thought. Without them I'd struggle," their creator admits.

The challenge facing organizations is to embrace the curious and holistic, the spiritual and the emotional, through new shapes and metaphors. "The traditional concept of organization is often desperately close to rigidification and compartmentalization rather than integration," says Tony Buzan. "The brain is self-organizing. It's designed to organize and manage knowledge. It has astonishing power to do that. It is in part a blank slate. If you feed it the incorrect formula it will organize itself in that way. This will lead to disorganization." Organizations must allow brains to self-organize. This requires that we move from physical gyms to develop brain gyms.

COMPASS LINKS
www.mind-map.com
www.designandhealth.com

TAKING BEARINGS
- How do you rate your corporate IQ, EQ and SQ?
- Do you visualize your thoughts by Mind Mapping?
- How do you train your brain?

Notes

1   Hock, Dee, *Birth of the Chaordic Age*, Berrett Koehler, San Francisco 1999
2   Hock, Dee, *Birth of the Chaordic Age*, Berrett Koehler, San Francisco 1999
3   Hock, Dee, *Birth of the Chaordic Age*, Berrett Koehler, San Francisco 1999
4   Strassmann, Paul, "Calculating knowledge capital," *Knowledge Management*, October 1999
5   Kleiner, Art and Roth, George, "How to make experience your company's best teacher," *Harvard Business Review*, September/October 1997. See also Steve Denning's work in this area.
6   Denning, Stephen, *The Springboard*, Butterworth, 2000
7   This has been systematized by Ikujiro Nonaka in his work – see Ikujiro, Nonaka; Krogh, Georg von; and Ichijo, Kazuo, *Enabling Knowledge Creation*, Oxford University Press, 2000
8   Snowden, David, "Knowledge management and storytelling," MITRE Technology Speakers Series, 2 June 2000
9   Reich, Robert, *Context Magazine*, September 2000
10 Arthur, Brian, "Increasing returns and the new world of business," *Harvard Business Review*, July–August 1996
11 Juanita developed these ideas in her Ph.D. thesis and in her book *The World Café*.
12 Nonaka, Ikujiro, and Takeuchi, Hirotaka, *The Knowledge-Creating Company*, Oxford University Press, 1995
13 Darius Mahdjoubi has explored the metaphorical allure of maps in his paper "Migration from business planning to innovation strategy by using the atlas of innovation."
14 Edvinsson, Leif, Beding, and Kitts, "Third generation of IC accounting," *Intellectual Capital Journal*, 2000
15 Mayo, Elton, *The Human Problems of an Industrial Civilization*, Viking, New York, 1960
16 Webber, Alan, "Learning for a change," *Fast Company*, May 1999
17 Brown, Tom, "Interview with Danah Zohar," FTDynamo.com
18 Perelman, Lewis, "Tom Stewart on intellectual capital," *Knowledge Inc.*, 1997
19 *Management review*
20 Ghoshal, Sumantra, and Bartlett, Christopher, "Beyond strategic planning to organization learning," *Strategy & Leadership*, Jan/Feb 1998
21 Quoted in Knowledge Leaders press release 13 November 2000
22 Hickins, Michael, "Xerox shares its knowledge," *Management Review*, September 1999
23 Stewart, Thomas, "Knowledge Worth $1.25 Billion," *Fortune*, Vol. 142, No. 13 November 27, 2000
24 Interview with Dan Tobin August 2001
25 Brown, John Seely, and Duguid, Paul, "Balancing act: How to capture knowledge without killing it," *Harvard Business Review*, May – June 2000
26 Brown, Tom, "Interview with Danah Zohar," FTDynamo.com; Zohar, Danah, SQ – Spiritual Intelligence, 2000; The Quantum Society, 1994

Workplaces Fit for Knowledge Workers

You are where you work.

KNOWLEDGE WORK SPACES

The famous Hawthorne Experiments into how people behave in a working environment took place at Western Electric's Hawthorne plant in Cicero, Illinois between 1927 and 1932. The researchers wanted to achieve an "intimate, habitual, intuitive familiarity with the phenomena."[1] This eventually produced over 20,000 interviews, which were diligently recorded and transcribed.

The Hawthorne studies began with experiments in which the lighting in the factory was altered. The hypothesis was that brighter light would raise morale and, as a result, increase productivity.

Hawthorne workers were separated into two groups. In one group the lighting levels were increased: productivity increased. In the other group the lighting remained at its normal level: productivity increased. Lighting levels were further increased, but still the productivity levels in the two groups remained much the same.

The researchers were confused, but returned with a more complicated experiment. In the factory's relay assembly test room, a group of six women who assembled telephone relay switches were selected and isolated in a test room. There they were diligently observed. Conditions were changed and tinkered with. But nothing seemed to reduce productivity.

The conclusion from the research team was that they had missed something. This something was the relationships, attention, attitudes, feelings, and perceptions of the people involved. The research program had revolved around selecting small groups of workers to be studied. This, not surprisingly, made them feel special. For the first time they actually felt that management was interested in them. The second effect was that the people felt like they belonged to a select team. They identified with their group. "The desire to stand well with one's fellows, the so-called human instinct of association, easily outweighs the merely individual interest and the logic of reasoning upon which so many spurious principles of management are based," commented Elton Mayo one of the leaders of the research.

The Harvard research team then determined to look more closely at how groups operated. Was their social structure behind the formation and behavior of such groups? The researchers chose the bank wiring room at the factory for this next stage in their experiments. This contained nine wiremen, three soldermen, two inspectors, and the observer.

The group appeared small and relatively simple to understand. But, the more the researchers looked at the group's behavior the more they uncovered.

The members of the group created a complex world of their own. They exerted control over it. Sometimes, their reasoning and perceptions were completely at odds with the truth. The researchers found that the workers did not, for example, understand the company's payment system. Misconceptions were handed down from one worker to the next and quickly became accepted as truth.

From an organizational perspective, the experiment in the bank wiring room provided a salutary lesson. It seemed that apparently well-organized and rigorously managed groups were nothing of the kind. Instead of being tightly controlled, easily regulated and understandable, they were a complex array of relationships and dynamic forces. If people worked together for any length of time, they formed their own status system, culture and structures which often served as protection against management.

Yet despite these findings, companies have carried on much as before. All this is from a personal, intellectual and organizational perspective disastrous. The opportunity cost of offices is huge. Culture and values are manifest in the worlds of work we create. And what disastrous worlds we continue to create.

Most organizations persist in treating people like cogs in a machine where managers operate the controls. Not only is it unproductive, it makes working life unnecessarily dull. Companies continue to squander their human capital. Look at the way they organize workers even today. Former Skandia CEO Björn Wolrath (now chairman of the Swedish organization Prevent which campaigns for workplace health) suggests that workers should demonstrate for a better working environment rather than just more money.

Just think of the ways in which we work and the places in which we work. In the UK, research found that the average size of a prison cell is 75 square feet. At some fashionable media companies the space allocated per employee is as little as 25 square feet. Open plan offices usually offer around 150 square feet. There is little space to move and no space to think.[2]

"For the sake of democracy and dignity we must encourage diversity and quality in work," says EU minister Mona Sahlin.[3] We need to create working space, which is sustainable.

Some companies have switched the lights on. (Sometimes literally. More and better lighting is recognized as a factor in aiding recovery rates in hospitals.) They understand that stimulating, fun environments produce results as well as motivated and happy people. They realize that knowledge is shared and multiplied in environments in which it can be easily shared. After all, as the Hawthorne studies proved, it's not that hard to do. Just allow people to switch on the lights and they will.[4]

At one of the ICA supermarkets in Sweden there was a problem with absenteeism. People complained of strain injuries. In response, ICA introduced ergonomically designed workstations at the tills. In addition, it brought in job rotation so that staff experienced different jobs in different parts of the store regularly. Training was stepped up. "The employees felt that the company took them and their problems seriously and that it was prepared to make a genuine effort to improve their work situation. The result was fewer strain injuries, and increased security and enjoyment at work. This meant, in turn, that the ICA workers also felt better as private individuals," concluded a report on workplace health.[5]

Making a difference usually requires that people have a degree of freedom. The Virginia-based IT consultancy Xperts gave its staff up to $1500 to cover the decoration of their own workspace.[6] Indeed, as well as mission statements, Tom Stewart suggests that companies also have permission statements, statements of the freedom granted to people:[7]

- Permission to think.
- Permission to reflect -- that is, to take a step back from the urgent and spend a day on the important.

- Permission to collaborate – within a department or outside it, without clearing it in advance.
- Permission to disagree.
- Permission to disagree strongly – that is, to say "screw you" without having to quit.
- Permission to invent.
- Permission to decide as best one can.
- Permission to be different.

Permission is being granted. In the quest for intelligent enterprising many are switching on the lights to create workplaces fit for knowledge workers.

Procter & Gamble The stereotypical old economy giant, consumer brands company Procter & Gamble launched an initiative called Organization 2005. The aim is to change the Cincinnati-based company from a bureaucratic behemoth into a fast-moving Internet savvy business. To speed up the process, the company has moved 3100 technical people (97 percent of its corporate IT staff) out of headquarters to work in product, market or business teams. The idea is that the technical experts will mingle with the rest of the organization, pollinating it with technical knowledge, which will add to its traditional marketing strengths.

Such changes do not necessarily please everyone. Organization 2005 did not boost the company's short-term performance – hardly surprising – and its instigator Durk Jager departed.

SAS Institute The lights are on full beam at the software company, SAS Institute, based in North Carolina. Its HQ includes a large gym (large enough for two basketball courts), a health clinic and day-care facilities. Other benefits include M&Ms distributed every week (employees may not like them, but it is something journalists always write about), massages, family benefits, a 35-hour week, live music in the canteen and so on.[8]

As you would expect if you had read motivational theorists from Douglas McGregor to Rosabeth Moss Kanter, SAS Institute is hugely successful. More to the point, in an age in which corporate loyalty is rare, SAS has a staff turnover rate of 3.7 percent. (The figure is not an aberration – it has never exceeded 5 percent.) As a result, it makes massive savings in recruitment and training costs – enough to pay for an awful lot of massages.

"SAS places enormous emphasis on three things: employees, customers, and products," said a *Fast Company* article on the company. "Employees and customers, for instance, are surveyed every year. The company says that 80 percent of the suggestions for product improvements that customers make most frequently eventually find their way into the software. SAS ploughs 30 percent or more of its revenue (that's revenue, not profit) back into R&D – a higher proportion than any other software company of its size." The message is that good business can be good for you and can be extraordinarily simple.

Viant Another company doing innovative things with its working space is the consulting firm Viant. At its Boston HQ it refers to creating a "leaky knowledge environment," an environment in which "knowledge accidents" occur as regularly as possible. Accidents must happen.

The chief effect of such humble-sounding initiatives is that they provide the environment and culture in which knowledge can be shared. Culture is the combined sum of the individual opinions, shared mindsets, values and norms (as defined by Hubert Saint-Onge). It is a component of organizational capital.

The workspace of tomorrow will be shaped in corporate culture and the mindset of knowledge workers. It is much more about Theory Y than Theory X. The new bottom line is in the workspace medium.

The management writer Louisa Wah combined my visions of the future workplace with those of Caela Farren, CEO of MasteryWorks and Jim O'Connell, vice president of Ceridian. The result was a ten point guide to tomorrow's workplace:

1. Knowledge workers will not have a traditional contractual relationship with employers. Instead, they will rent their professional skills and knowledge on a "freelance" basis to different companies at different times.

2. The corporate headquarters will evolve into "heart centers", where emotional intelligence fuels creativity, innovation and an enterprising spirit.

3. Downsizing, upsizing, rightsizing, growth and stabilization will all be welcome forms of "sizing" companies. People will have coping mechanisms that prepare them for any shift.
4. In the 24/7 global environment, productivity will be driven by speed and efficiency rather than the number of staff hours dedicated to a project.
5. Internet-speed workplaces will radically transform the world of work, making work across multiple time zones and irregular schedules more and more common.
6. People won't work for organizations where they don't get a share of the profits and where work/life balance is not a given.
7. Companies will no longer decide which benefits an employee needs. Instead, employees will log on to their company's web site to customize their benefits programs.
8. People will feel an increasing ownership of their destinies, lives and careers. "Living skills" will be just as important as "professional skills."
9. The boundaries between work and school will blur. Learning will be centered more around professions and trades, and there will be more mentor/apprentice relationships, with Internet-based coaching provided by people one has never met.
10. A digital divide will emerge, separating employees who are tech-savvy and those who aren't. Smart companies will invest more in human capital and become virtual universities to narrow that gap.[9]

That was two years ago. Things have been moved on, but the trends remain much the same.

COMPASS LINKS
www.viant.com
www.sasinstitute.com
www.creativityatwork.com
www.gurteen.com
www.bottomline.se
www.designandhealth.com
www.prevent.se

TAKING BEARINGS
- How do you describe your working environment?
- What permission statements do you have for your knowledge workers?
- Who is in charge of the architecture of your workplace?
- How do you promote workplace health for your knowledge workers?

PLACES WITH SENSE

Another form of compass is a Chinese luo pan. Extraordinarily precise and beautiful, these are the chief instruments of feng shui. The compasses contain a legion of formulas and secrets to enable the feng shui expert to examine a space. Flaky nonsense? You might think so, but feng shui is another type of accounting, another means of measuring and making sense of things.

It must be said that there is a lot of work for someone armed with a luo pan in the average office building. Offices have a lengthy history of repressing pleasure, fulfilment and creativity. First, there was the Victorian stereotype of desks arranged in lines with clerks toiling away. This evolved into the modern stereotype of office workers staring at screens in anonymous cubicles. The angst and political strife of cubicle life is accurately captured by Scott Adams in his Dilbert cartoon strip.

The Dilbert-led revolt against cubicle life has not yet improved working life. Office life lives on. For some, the reasons behind this have more to do with Machiavelli than organizational efficiency. "For corporations to get employees to increase productivity, they need to exercise power over them," says Gerry Griffin, author of *The Power Game*. "The organization of workspace is the way in which the corporation seeks to do this. Many think that their workspace is a reflection of how far they have progressed up the organization. The big corner office is something to aim towards. In fact, your workspace is an expression of the current power relations which exist between you and the corporation."[10]

With such power games at work, permutations come and go. Desks are always being re-shuffled; offices re-designed; spaces re-designated. Rarely does this involve senior managers having smaller offices. The most recent fashion has been for hot-desking. From a cost point of view this is laudable. Employees have no fixed workplace. Desks do not stand idle. Hot-desking effectively utilizes infrastructure resources. The downside of this is that people are, in an office sense, nomadic. They no longer even have a cubicle of their own. For some, this is the worst of every world, an awkward deskless limbo whose financial efficiency is offset by cutting the essential emotional and practical relationship-building ties of office life.

If offices are to thrive in the future, the challenge is to create offices that work, that reflect knowledge work and social relationships. This is not something office designers have a very good track record at creating. Most obviously, modern offices struggle with the notion of teamworking – hardly a new and original idea. The balance between teamworking and providing peace and quiet to do concentrated work is difficult, usually impossible. Research by BOSTI Associates, an American office research organization, posed a simple question: "If 75 to 95 percent of all workers need to do undistracted solo work, why are 75 percent in acoustically-porous workspaces?"

Laurence Lyons, editor of *Rethinking Business Space*, suggests we need to move away from the very notion of the office. "Business space is the name for the new place where white-collar work gets done," says Lyons. "The old name – office space – has become too restricting. Office space was built around an organizational hierarchy that physically anchored people close to an office manager or supervisor in some fixed location."[11] In an increasingly mobile working world, such notions are fast being consigned to history.

Dr Lyons suggests that the new generation of managers are already shaping the spaces they inhabit. "Business space is emerging around a thoughtful new breed of leader who typically contributes to a high-performance network, or works within a diverse yet cohesive team. These successful people thrive **We need to move away from the very notion of the office.** on results. They have learned to replace the old hierarchical structure with their own merit-based system in which individual freedom and team responsibility are prized." All they have to lose are their cubicles.

For another glimpse of the future, consider the London-based advertising agency St Luke's. The firm has embarked on a radical experiment. According to Andy Law, St Luke's chairman: "The aim is to operate in the 'creative age' rather than the 'industrial age'. It's all about being comfortable with chaotic, almost anarchic, ways of working, which frees employees to be creative and to work in a non-linear way."

Staff at the agency have no desks of their own. Between meetings, they hot-desk – taking a seat at any one of the computer stations they share communally. Telephones are radio-based and small enough to fit into a pocket. Calls follow employees from place to place.

Client meetings are held in brand rooms. Once a client signs up with the agency, they are allocated a conference room which is fitted out in the style and culture of the brand, and which they can use whenever they choose, calling on St Luke's staff as required.

Underpinning its management philosophy is a new sort of corporate structure. Andy Law says the company wants to start a revolution. "We're fundamentally convinced that there is a connection between co-ownership, creativity, collaboration, and competitive advantage," he says. "Many people here have given up untold riches and power to pursue this experiment."

The role of art in the office environment is also increasingly taken seriously. Visit Unilever's UK headquarters in London's Blackfriars and it resembles an art gallery such are the artistic wonders on display. Major corporations are increasingly embracing the notion of art for art's sake.

Few can match the collection assembled by the Deutsche Bank. It now owns 48,000 works – and is involved in countless exhibitions and art projects as well as the Deutsche Guggenheim exhibition hall in Berlin. Its London HQ includes a relatively meagre collection of 2,500 works. The Bank's collection has been assembled since the 1970s as, says the Bank, "part of its responsibility as an enterprise and towards society." The aim is to buy relatively inexpensive works to support artists rather than investing in expensive works. The average Deutsche Bank purchase costs £800. The company organizes tours of its collection for employees and clients.

Major corporations are increasingly embracing the notion of art for art's sake.

What links these various companies is a sensitivity to the environment. They think about the environment constantly. Space is regarded by them not as a vacuum but as a creative possibility. They recognize that little things make the difference. They believe in contactivity – a meeting that goes beyond connectivity and creates both contact and meeting of minds leading to knowledge activity.

But there is more than one sense. Think of the sense of smell and remember the scents of Skandia's Future Center – tar, cinnamon and vanilla. It is common sense. It makes the place smell good and distinctive, and it makes a huge difference. It is about releasing the power of innovation and tacit knowledge.[12]

Indeed, the sense of smell is emotionally incredibly powerful. It is also highly personal. Hundreds of years ago, professional perfumers would create special scents for affluent individuals. The perfume – or at least some of the elements of it – were passed from one generation to the next.

Dutch psychologist Piet Vroon's *Smell: The Secret Seducer*, puts the case for the nose and examines why odor-evoked memories are unusually emotionally potent. The sensation of an odor persists for greater lengths of time than do sensations of vision or audition.

Vroon points out that only two synapses separate the olfactory nerve from the amygdala, which is involved in experiencing emotion and also in emotional memory. In addition, only three synapses separate the olfactory nerve from the hippocampus, which is implicated in memory, especially

The smell of cinnamon buns is particularly good at evoking happiness.

working memory and short-term memory. Olfaction is the sensory modality that is physically closest to the limbic system, of which the hippocampus and amygdala are a part, and which is responsible for emotions and memory.

"Western cultures have had a love–hate relationship with the sense of smell," says Vroon. "And if we look at the war waged nowadays in the commercials over sanitary pads, tampons, diapers for infants and adults, sweet-smelling soaps, skin-care products, deodorants, perfumes and the like, we can say that smell is considered important once again."

Alice Isen, professor of marketing at Cornell's Johnson School of Business, has conducted extensive research into what causes people to have more positive moods. Among her discoveries was that the smell of cinnamon buns is particularly good at evoking happiness. Americans appear to be paying attention. Cinnamon sales are rapidly increasing and the American Spice Trade Association says that cinnamon is now the spice "routinely described as favorite," by Americans.

So important is the sense of smell that artificial noses have been developed (by car companies among others). At the University of Illinois researchers hope that its nose could be used to find counterfeit perfumes, at customs checks to find banned substances, and to sniff out poisons and toxins in factories.

And there is also the rise of what is called "sensory marketing" which recognizes that smells are integral parts of the consumer experience.

The logic is simple. If you walk past a baker's shop you will be enticed by the smell of freshly baked bread. Suddenly, you will feel the need to purchase a freshly baked loaf.

The power of air means that a number of companies are now creating their own scents and pumping them through the air conditioning. The shirt maker Thomas Pink has the smell of freshly laundered linen piped into its shops. Supermarket chains waft the aroma of freshly baked bread through their stores. The retail chain Woolworth's filled some of its UK stores with the alluring aromas of mulled wine in a pre-Christmas experiment. Tesco has developed its own brand smell.

Smells may also soon be travelling by cyberspace. "Digital scent technology is the biggest revolution in food technology since refrigeration!" proclaims the convincingly colorful web site for DigiScents. The idea behind DigiScents is to transmit smells via the Internet. Its technology is labelled iSmell. Forget bricks and clicks, think clicks and sniffs. The company has a vice president of scentography – try explaining that when someone asks, "What do you do?". But there is nothing fishy about DigiScents as a business. It has a strategic alliance with Procter & Gamble and a host of endorsements.

Intellectual capital is about such skill in cultivating relationships.

Smell matters because companies need to create cultures and environments in which people make contact with each other. The important difference is between connecting and contacting people.

Connectivity is often talked about. But it's really a mechanical thing. You are connected if your PC is linked to the Internet, but that is not necessarily creating anything worthwhile. Contactivity is more important. An eighteenth century Italian economist summed it up neatly when he observed that "value is a relation between persons." Intellectual capital is about such skill in cultivating relationships.

Organizations must create environments and cultures which enable relationships to be built and cultivated – between people inside and outside.

COMPASS LINKS
www.fluidminds.com
www.futurecenter.dk
www.prevent.se
www.steelcase.com

TAKING BEARINGS
- What does your organization smell of?
- How do people personalize their working environment? What about you?
- How does your working environment help you behave more innovatively?
- How does your working environment add to the cultivation of relationships and contactivity?
- On whose job description do you find responsibility for smell and sense making in your organization?

PLACES WITH MEANING

As the Hawthorne researchers found, work is a social experience. Building an effective "social ecology," Anil K. Gupta and Vijay Govindarajan – two US-based business academics – have observed, is a crucial requirement for effective knowledge management.[13] They define social ecology as the social environment in which people operate.[14]

The experience of Nucor Steel is instructive. The company is not a child of the new economy. Far from it. In fact, it is in the distinctly old economy business of steel. But Nucor Corp. has been the world's fastest-growing and most innovative steel company for the past three decades. Nucor has used knowledge management to build its main strategic competencies: plant construction and start-up; manufacturing processes; and the rapid adoption of new technologies ahead of the competition.

Nucor has used financial inventiveness to boost employee expertise and also "share the pain" programs to share work loss equally in recessions, thus stimulating loyalty. It has also proved excellent at the tasks associated with sharing and mobilizing knowledge: identifying opportunities to share knowledge and encouraging employees to do so; building effective transmission channels; and convincing individuals to accept and use knowledge received.

Nucor has used a number of instruments to achieve this: sharing best practice through routine measurement and distribution of performance data; paying incentives to work groups rather than individuals to reward sharing; keeping individual plants small to encourage the face-to-face transfer of unstructured knowledge; and transferring people between different plants.

Gupta and Govindarajan suggest ways other companies can emulate Nucor's success. These include: setting "stretch goals;" providing incentives; cultivating a sense of empowerment; allowing every unit to experiment in a "sandbox;" and developing an internal market for the exchange of ideas.

These factors could be abbreviated to a simple, single call to arms: give people meaning. People crave meaning. They want to feel that they belong to something, that their efforts and talents are appreciated. It's less about scent and more about sense.

Successful knowledge economy companies have created their own distinctive cultures. In part, this is a response to the natural human desire to belong – the need for meaning. At Skandia, the former CEO initiated a very successful values-based program called Ideas for Life. According to Brian Hall of Values Technologies the core of knowledge is your values.

The online brokerage firm E★Trade, for example, has its own way of initiating new recruits. CEO Christos Cotsakos insists that all new arrivals, including senior managers, stand on a chair in front of 40 or so employees and "reveal something about themselves." Faced with the unusual rite of passage, one normally reserved Englishman surprised himself by pulling a penknife from his pocket and slicing off the expensive Hermes tie he was wearing. The symbolic cutting of the traditional business shackles speaks volumes. Culture can be liberating.

Cutting ties is fine but real belonging is created through strongly held values, which are authentically believed within the organization. Anyone can cut ties; you can't fake values.

Knowledge economy companies try to express their values in various ways. Amazon.com, for example, famously has its six core values: customer obsession; ownership; bias for action; frugality; a high hiring bar; and innovation. These it hopes provide the spring-board for its vision as "the world's most customer-centric company. The place where people come to find and discover anything they might want to buy on line." Skandia's Jan Carendi talked of the five Fs – fast, fun, flexible, freedom, friendly.

Companies like Amazon claim to offer a new sense of meaning and purpose to working life. They recognize that the new generation of workers want more than just a pay check at the end of the month. They want meaning and purpose. Since the early days, Amazon has had the stated aim of revolutionizing business. Its values are part of the appeal. "It's like the Cultural Revolution meets Sam Walton. It's dotcommunism," one magazine observed.

Among those converted to the importance of values is David Pottruck the president and co-CEO of the brokerage firm Charles Schwab. In *Clicks and Mortar*, the book Pottruck co-wrote with Schwab colleague Terry Pearce, he outlines the importance of values in the "passion driven growth" of the firm.

Recalling the decision to write down the Schwab values, he says: "Until then, it hadn't dawned on us that the firm had gotten big enough that we needed to communicate the fundamentals of the culture explicitly. In a way it was like the drafting of the Declaration of Independence. It put in writing what we understood to be the truths of our company, truths that we had been operating with for a number

Workers want more than just a pay check at the end of the month.

of years, but that could now stand as a beacon to guide our actions not just as a company but as individuals within that company."

The entire management team worked on the project. Eventually five core values were agreed: fairness, empathy, teamwork, and responsiveness, constantly striving to be worthy of our customers' trust. "We set out to etch the vision and values we believed to be our cultural DNA into the mind and heart of every Schwab employee," Pottruck says.

So why the sudden outbreak of values? "What you are is becoming just as important as what you sell. The values that corporations stand for are increasingly affecting their ability to hire the best people and sell their products. There is an awakening awareness that there is a causal link between the rapidly escalating environmental and social issues and the philosophy of business," says Richard

Barrett, former values co-ordinator at the World Bank.[15] Brian Hall at Values Technologies takes this even further by suggesting that knowledge *is* values.

Values are also seen as a way to attract bright people to growing businesses. Take de Baer Corporate Clothing, for example. Founded by chief executive Jacqueline de Baer, the company designs and manufactures natty staff uniforms which interpret the brands of the likes of Holiday Inn, Boots Opticians and the Odeon Cinema in Leicester Square.

As befits its stylish products, de Baer sees itself as an international company with personality. It aims to create a culture that will attract young talent looking for an informal and fun environment to work in. The company's values include fun, integrity, openness and learning.

"For us it's been incredibly important," says Jacqueline de Baer. "If you start a company then the company takes on a lot of your personality. As it gets bigger it's very important to identify the personality of the company. It might still be 75 percent the personality of the founder but there may be other elements. Defining the values is very powerful. The values can guide you in all sorts of ways, especially in speeding up decision making. We are very clear on what we are trying to do."

The company also uses values to guide recruitment decisions. Every new person to join at management level has a telephone interview to discuss their values before being asked to the first formal interview. At other levels within the organization, questions aimed at identifying values are incorporated into the first interview. "It's more than just empowering decision making. I recruit against the values," says Jacqueline de Baer.

Values may be popular with up-and-coming companies, but they are not a new idea. The fact is that they have been a staple of successful organizations for centuries. Well-managed companies have always found it useful to spell out what they stand for. The fact is that a set of core values underpins many of the most famous and long-lived of the old economy companies. The more networked and partnership-oriented the enterprise becomes the more essential is the need for explicit values.

General Electric, one of the outstanding old economy success stories of recent times subscribes to a set of core values. Among them are "setting stretch goals," and "simplicity." Others organizations that find it helpful to spell out their core values include Clarica, Walt Disney, the US Army, and the Federal Bureau of Investigation. Siemens has developed online mapping of its values based on Brian Hall's research.

There are two issues surrounding values. First, while companies can be created instantly, cultures are not created overnight. "Anyone who has tried to create a culture ... knows it can't be done on Internet time. Cultures aren't designed. They simmer; they fester; they brew continually, evolving their particular temperament as people learn what kind of behavior works or doesn't work in the particular company," says Art Kleiner.

Second, corporate values can be seen as a form of corporate brainwashing.

The line between brainwashing and belief is a narrow one, but there has to be belief for anything and any organization to thrive. The lack of values can prove costly – look at Shell's experiences and the HIV campaign against the pharmaceutical companies in South Africa.

Successful companies will be those that unite the internal company culture and the external market position through a shared set of beliefs. This is what the Danish branding expert Jesper Kunde calls a corporate religion. "The word religion derives from the Latin *religare* – to bind something together in a common expression," Kunde says. "Corporate religion is that which expresses the soul of a company and supports the building of a strong market position. In order to make a corporate religion come alive you have to describe your internal organization as well as your external market. These internal values create an internal movement which delivers the whole heart and soul of the company."

Companies can be created instantly, cultures are not created overnight.

According to Kunde: "Companies must be able to describe themselves – both internally and externally – because they are no longer adequately defined by the products they make. Customers buy the company and everything it stands for. So the company must be able to define itself in a connected and coherent way."

One challenge is that companies are not very good at explaining their tacit dimensions. They express themselves in terms of products and numbers. "I talk to board members and the key problem is that they are afraid of giving a little bit of themselves," says Kunde. "They think it's dangerous. But people – employees and customers – want to know who they are dealing with. We want to know the attitude of management. You cannot expect to attract young people unless you tell them what you're all about."

Kunde points to Richard Branson's Virgin Group as an example of how to create a corporate religion. "Branson is a true visionary who sticks to his faith. He has amply demonstrated that you can market a wide range of product categories under one brand. In other words the value element of the brand – what the company stands for – is elevated over the product."

Intelligent enterprising has a spiritual dimension. This is not a form of brainwashing; this is a sense of context and meaning. The spiritual dimension elevates work to a different level. Organizations have addressed the how of work. They have even begun to get to grips with the emotional and social aspects. But what they have largely failed to articulate is why we work.

COMPASS LINKS
www.niwl.se
www.knowledgeecology.com
www.valuestech.com
www.saint-ongetoolkit.com

TAKING BEARINGS
- What are your enterprising values?
- Does your organization attract investors, customers, talent, and partners against those values?
- How do you shape new innovative partnerships based on values?

Notes

1 Roethlisberger, Fritz, *The Elusive Phenomena* (ed. Lombard, George), Harvard University Press, Cambridge, 1977

2 DTZ Research, September 2000

3 Work Life Conference, Malmö, Sweden, January 2001

4 Research is going on at the Karolinska Institute in Stockholm on the impact of architecture at work.

5 Thomsson, Helene, and Menckel, Ewa, "What is workplace health promotion?", *Prevent* 1997

6 Hammonds, Keith, "My cubicle, my self," *Fast Company*, September 2000

7 Stewart, Thomas A., "Just think: No permission needed," *Fortune*, Vol. 143, No. 1, January 8, 2001

8 Fishman, Charles, "Sanity Inc.," *Fast Company* January 1999

9 Wah, Louisa, "Workplace of the future," *Management Review*, 1999

10 Griffin, Gerry, *The Power Game*, Capstone, 1999

11 Interview with Stuart Crainer 2000

12 See Nonaka Ichijo and Von Grogh's, *Enabling Knowledge Creation*, Oxford University Press, 2000, on how to unlock the mystery of tacit knowledge.

13 Anil K Gupta, and Vijay Govindarajan, "Knowledge management's social dimension: lessons from Nucor Steel," *Sloan Management Review*, Vol. 42, No. 1, Fall 2000

14 George Puv, now at INSEAD, developed an Internet community around knowledge ecology.

15 Barrett, Richard, "Liberating your soul," www.corptools.com

U-capital & I-commerce

We are what we visualize.

DIRECTIONS DIFFER

The sinan looks like a spoon on top of a board. Rotate this ancient Chinese instrument and it spins around. Eventually, its handle comes to rest. Unlike a Western compass which points to the north, ancient Chinese compasses always pointed south.

As an enhancement to the sinan, the Chinese scientist Zu Chongzi developed a compass which was attached to a vehicle so that travellers would be ensured of knowing the direction in which they were travelling. Later, by the Song Dynasty, a "south-pointing fish compass" had been invented. This consisted of a carved wooden fish with a magnet embedded in its body. A needle was attached to the magnet and protruded out of the fish's mouth. The fish was usually placed in a dish of water and would swivel around till it came to rest pointing southward. One of the variations of the south-pointing fish was the south-pointing turtle which consisted of a carved wooden turtle that swiveled on a stand.

Intellectual capital is individual capital, the capital which resides within our individual brains.

All this goes to prove that one man's south is another's north. Our keenness to know where we are going is eternal and universal. Yet the directions in which we travel differ from individual to individual. We are masters of our own journeys and are always nearer by not keeping still.

We are fellow travellers. On my business card I label myself a Global Knowledge Nomad (another version has me as a Knowledge Viking). Like many executives throughout the world, my life is nomadic. I have a base in Stockholm, a home, friends, family, contacts, acquaintances. Yet, I spend a great deal of my time travelling. I criss-cross the Atlantic, pop down to Italy for the day, always on the move. So, I am nomadic – a very modern incarnation of the Vikings of history. My journeys are truly global.

What drives me? Why am I sitting in business class lounges connecting through my mobile phone? Why am I working on my laptop at 30,000 feet above the icy Atlantic?

What drives me is curiosity, navigating and exploring the world of knowledge. And so I travel asking questions in the quest for more useful, enlightening and meaning making insights.[1]

So far, I have talked of corporations and organizations and the role of people within them. But at the heart of all this, all these notions of intellectual capital and knowledge economics, are individuals; people charged with shaping their own destinies, careers and lives. Intellectual capital is individual capital, the capital which resides within our individual brains and potential.

More than ever before, the onus is on us as individuals to nurture our own innate abilities, our talent, and to supplement them where and when necessary. "Of all the great historical revolutions, I prefer the Internet Age – because it's a revolution of the mind," says former Microsoft chief technology officer and co-founder of Intellectual Ventures, Nathan Myhrvold. "The new economy is about rethinking and reshaping what has already happened. It's about producing fertile ground for radically new ideas. Workers with good ideas, or the ability to generate ideas, can write their own ticket. We're talking about the democratization of power."[2]

The desire for self-fulfillment is incredibly strong. We want to take power. It is a universal force. We have to take the initiative to release our talent potential. Some already have.

One of the select few is Tony Buzan who is intent on maximizing the potential of his own brain. He uses his own mind mapping techniques to plan his itinerary. To some the detail of his personal planning may seem excessive. But it is important because it is him exercising his choice.

Buzan took control of his destiny during his time at university. "I was one of the best note takers in school and university," he explains. "We took standard linear notes and were trained to use certain ink, Quink blue-black. A blue or a black is monochrome, a monotone is monotonous and dull. The bulk of the literate population is taking notes in terms of knowledge management, which send them to sleep and which may bring only a small fraction of what the brain needs. It was a long painful and very exciting discovery."

To some, Tony's regime of charts and different coloured lines may appear excessive self-management. He thinks otherwise:

"It doesn't feel organized. It is a natural expression of my self-organizing system. I plan beyond the end of my life and then go back from that. I plan comfortably a year ahead, two really. I plan at the end and beginning of the day. I don't plan weekly, but daily and monthly.

"I'm very much not a control freak. I'm flexible in changing what I've decided if it fits in with my goals. Planning is not control. If I'm thinking ten years ahead, it is a freedom. Freedom to make my own decisions and enjoy myself.

"It used to take me three months to do a 5000 word essay. That was a lot of writing and rewriting and was the same for the other students. If a writer writes 500 words a day then they're pleased. It made sense to me, but then I thought that was a page and a bit, four minutes of talking. Then I began to see that it was utterly insane. In writing, my function is to transfer what I know from my head onto the page. I learned to type and got up to 70 words a minute. My fingers were tripping over my thoughts all the time. I thought there must be a faster way.

"What is the fastest most durable muscle in my body? The tongue. I took mind maps and taped what I would have typed. I have a mind map for a book surrounded by other mind maps. I spend two days getting myself into writing/grammatical mode – as we never speak in grammar mode. I then translate the mind maps into text.

"My average writing per day is 10,000 to 20,000 words. It doesn't feel fast. The mind map is the framework. I don't need to change it. It is the thinking that leads to the mind map. When I'm writing I have a mind map in my head. I describe it. I know how many words I put down – 140 to 150 words a minute. Give me 30 minutes and I know how much I can produce."

Buzan's methods mean that he has now written over 80 books. There is a lot more to be done. "I'm increasing my output because I've got so many things to say," he says. "When you know the potential of the brain, it's profound and profoundly important. But if you've never been taught about your brain all you know is that your brain is your real problem. It is three pounds of grey slush and you're losing brain cells and your memory's going. People don't like their brains, they've been taught the formula that colour, imagination and day dreaming are wrong and childish. So when someone comes along and says you need to use color and be playful, the immediate reaction is that they're talking nonsense. It's not just teaching people how to do it. It is removing the blindness with which people have been brought up.

"Most people think that they're less able to determine their own future than they really are. People think they're trapped when they are not. It is self-perpetuating until you get a bigger perspective. Once you realize you are trapped you change."

Giving our brains the opportunity to release their potential is a complex and enormous challenge. Can you?

COMPASS LINKS
www.mind-map.com

TAKING BEARINGS
- Do you cultivate your talent?
- How do you visualize and brand your talent?
- In what direction is the cultivation of your talent travelling?
- How do you apply Mind Mapping or similar techniques to navigate your brain potential?

BRAIN STRESS

"Mind productivity … is highly conditioned by the culture of the workplace, the vision and purpose of the work, the alignment of personal and corporate values, and the meaning the work brings to the individual's life. Mind productivity is also conditioned by what is taking place in an individual's life outside of work. When an individual is preoccupied with family issues or changes that are taking place in their life, such as a divorce or a death in the family, mind productivity goes down. Mind productivity is also affected by constant meetings or travel. Long quiet moments are needed for the mind to switch into its full potential," says Richard Barrett, former values co-ordinator at the World Bank.[3] This is also called brain stilling by Professor Chakraborty of the Indian Management Institute in Calcutta.

Modern executive life takes little heed of mind productivity. Knowledge workers travel physically and need also to travel intellectually, but organizations remain intent on believing that quantity of work comes before quality. The phenomenon of brain stress – often called burnout – has long been recognized. Employees who work too hard for too long can become demotivated, depressed and in extreme cases suffer nervous breakdowns. For the twenty-first-century knowledge worker, surrounded by complex technology, brain stress is a constant reality, a humbling reminder of our fallibility as well as the source of our individualism.

According to research, brain stress results in less innovative thought processing.

According to Swedish research, brain stress results in less innovative thought processing. Brain stress, therefore, has a serious impact on individual and collective intellectual capital.[4]

The stimulus for the stress is obvious. According to Juliet Schor, economist and author of *The Overworked American*, employees now routinely work an additional month per annum compared with 20 years ago. But the extra time doesn't necessarily benefit sustainable value creation. We need much more knowledge care than knowledge management.

We work long hours and now more of us work. The Families and Work Institute calculates that the percentage of dual-income families in the US increased from 66 percent in 1977 to 78 percent in 1998. These families are generally rich in financial capital but poor in time to nourish their intellectual capital.

Little wonder then that dreams of a balanced lifestyle remain just that. "My family has been … extremely tolerant of the fact that I haven't been there much for the last ten years," Viant chief Bob Gett told *Fast Company*. "This is sad, but I have resigned myself to the fact that I will never be able to enjoy any significant quality time until after I retire."[5]

A five-year tracking study by the University of Manchester Institute of Science and Technology found that over 80 percent of executives worked over 40 hours a week and one in ten worked over 60 hours. A resounding – though depressing – 86 percent said that the long hours had an affect on their relationship with their children and 71 percent said that it damaged their health.

Today's knowledge workers need a better balance between professional and personal lives. That's what technology is for. Technology gives us more time. It used to take seven hours of work to produce one litre of milk. Now it takes seven minutes. Apply the same principle to the world of knowledge work and life should be a lot better than it is. Technology can be used to reduce lead times for peak performance.

"We should work smarter not harder. The key is to focus on doing things that you are better at doing than the competition," says Jonas Ridderstråle. "Another element to this is the blurring of divides between home and work. If our work is done using our brain we are talking about a 168-hour working week. Work is no longer a place, it is an activity."

Yet how many organizations create situations in which people can experiment, prototype or even change their lifestyles? Not many.

In a *Fast Company* article, Christoph Niemann examined the career and life choices we have to make.[6] He began by quoting Freud: "It is impossible to escape the impression that people commonly use false standards of measurement – that they seek power, success and wealth for themselves and admire them in others, and that they underestimate what is of true value in life." (False standards of measurement are also applied elsewhere, as we have seen.)

Freud was right. A survey conducted by *Fast Company* with Roper Starch Worldwide of 1,096 people proved the point. An impressive 91 percent of the respondents said that "making their personal lives more of a priority was important to them." They were then given a hypothetical choice: a $10,000 pay rise or an extra hour a day at home in the bosom of their cherished family. No contest: 83 percent chose the dollar bills.

Brain stress is either not regarded as a problem or seen as someone else's responsibility. "Burnout is the outcome of a mismatch between workers and the workplace," say Michael P. Leiter and Christina Maslach, authors of *The Truth About Burnout*. "A critical point about burnout which is often missed is that it is a management problem, not simply an individual one. Too often managers side-step the issue as being either outside of their mandate or impossible to address." In reality, a fundamental leadership issue faced in intellectual capital is to deal with the issue of knowledge care.

Professor Andrew Kakabadse at the UK's Cranfield School of Management, has also investigated the phenomenon of burnout as part of a world wide study of top executive performance. His data, based on a detailed survey of 6,500 managers from ten countries, suggests all leaders are prone to burnout, but their organizations are often embarrassed by the phenomenon and don't know what to do about it.

"Corporate life requires deadlines to be met and inevitably workloads are unevenly shared, meaning that organizations generate their share of workaholics irrespective of the wishes of the individual," he says. "In addition, organizational chaos is rife, yet most workplaces still implicitly demand employees be 'corporate people', living and dreaming about attaining success in organizational life."

Serious attention, Professor Kakabadse says, should be given to how burnout happens, how to recognize and cope with it and how to combat it. The symptoms include: increasing fatigue; not listening effectively; feeling saturated with work; feeling unable to participate in routine operational conversations.

What makes the telltale signs hard to spot, however, is that declining morale and feelings of personal vulnerability usually emerge slowly and insidiously. "Increases in stress, job pressure, competition, higher work complexity, faster pace of life and the greater likelihood of redundancy all make for an inevitable drip, drip of negativity which leads many top managers to burnout," says Professor Kakabadse.

The problem is compounded in companies with a macho culture where caffeine rather than reason is used to cover the body's signals of fatigue. Ambitious young managers can become obsessed with keeping their plates spinning to the detriment of their health. Flatter organizations mean fewer promotions, with people stuck in the same job for longer periods, especially in the public sector.

"Prolonged demotivation leads to an emotional deterioration which is worsened by a realization that to some extent current lifestyle traps us in our jobs," says Professor Kakabadse. "Age, difficulty in matching remuneration packages and the continuity needed to support family life contribute to a sense of being trapped."

It is often worse for those further down the organization. Evidence suggests that stress is more pronounced among those who are not in control of their own destiny. If people are just an employment number they are unlikely to feel any sense of commitment. Those without a knowledge identity of their own, need to acquire a knowledge compass and start nourishing their identity assets.

But brain stress does not have to be part of organizational life. We now know more about the circumstances in which the brain flourishes than ever before. The trouble is that old organizational perspectives do not reflect the leaps forward we have made. Research suggests that the knowledge workers can work at peak levels for only two to four hours a day. Meanwhile, labor regulations remain fixated with the eight hour working day.

COMPASS LINKS

www.fastcompany.com
www.ceos.nu
www.designandhealth.com
www.hiwl.se
www.alphabiotics.com

TAKING BEARINGS

- What does knowledge care mean to you?
- How balanced is your working life? Would your partner/colleagues agree?
- Where do you find space for brain stilling?
- What indicators of measurement are used in your organization to capture the issues of brain stress, knowledge care and brain productivity?

BUILDING IDENTITY ASSETS

Career management is not a new phenomenon. What is, is who is in control. In the distant past, life unrolled before you. It was largely not yours to control. Then, during the twentieth century, the corporation (through the HR department) emerged as the determiner of careers. Now, careers will be increasingly managed by individuals. It is we, as individuals, as Me Inc., who make the choices and search for the employers of our talents. In other words human capital is in search of structural capital.

The objective of all this is simple enough. Health and happiness comes from working at what we are good at and in ways that suit our abilities. The trouble is that this rarely happens. The reason, says

Peter Drucker, is because we often have little idea of what we are good at.[7]

Identity assets

The route to outstanding performance is to identify and improve your unique skills, and then to find jobs, or assignments, which match those skills, values etc. Ask questions, find the answers, and then you are equipped to make the right decisions for your career – and life – development. We have to identify our identity assets, visualize, and develop them as trademarks and add new assets as we go.

This is what Paul Strassmann calls Personal Knowledge Capital (PKC). "PKC is directly related to the total compensation a knowledge worker can obtain in the marketplace. We can calculate the relationship between an individual's PKC and salary on the assumption that employers 'rent' a person's PKC. This approach discards classical theories about wages and sees individuals themselves as capitalists," says Strassman.[8] He has also developed the notion of corporate knowledge capital (CKC) – "reflected in the worth of corporate earnings to shareholders."

This is also amplified in recent research by Baruch Lev who found a strong correlation between stockholder value and variable reward systems.

Another approach comes from Mick Cope, author of *Know Your Own Value?*, who provides a practical means – the knowledge profile or "K-profile" – for assessing what you know as an individual and working out how much it is worth to others.[9] As Cope, following Charles Handy, points out, it is increasingly the case that people can extract more market value out of selling one hour of their knowledge then selling one hour of their physical time.

This is the concept of "personal capital." Now most companies will often not understand the value of personal capital, and will almost certainly undervalue it. It is therefore up to the individual to understand what he or she is worth and demand the market value.

"The age of the knowledge individual has arrived with a vengeance," writes Cope. "This is because ultimately, learning and knowledge will be discovered and delivered by individuals, not faceless corporate bodies. Hence, if individuals are not motivated to acquire or trade knowledge, then little learning can or will take place at an organizational level. The critical issue is to recognize the significance of the individual's role and value in enhancing the value of personal capital within any modern business."

Cope divides knowledge (both tacit and explicit) into three simplified cognitive areas, which he labels head, hand and heart. In this system:

- Head indicates thought processing;
- Hand indicates how we act, behave, or physically interact with the world;
- Heart indicates the emotions that we use to manage ourselves and our relationships with others.

Cope writes: "In the vast majority of cases we draw upon all three currencies to create value in the marketplace [though] it is likely that one of them will take a dominant role."

Cope's notion of a personal "K-profile" is essentially a matrix of tacit and explicit knowledge (each subdivided into head, heart, and hand) on one side and what Cope calls the "knowledge stock and flow framework (discover, delay, dispose, diffuse, and deliver)" on the other.

How much use the K-profile can be put to in real life is probably down to what each individual makes of it. But there can be little doubt that in setting out a way of codifying what Me Inc. is worth, the message is simple: don't undersell your talent, develop your knowledge brand and identity asset.

Reinventing your job

I asked Tony Buzan how he would label himself. He replied: "I think as a poet, author and businessman. Holanthropy is a word I have devised – the study of the mind and body, intra- and inter-personal relationships." How would you describe yourself?

People need to take charge of their knowledge life. They can start by taking charge of their current job and everyone's perception of their current job. If your job is important enough to spend 50 hours a week on, take control. This is part of building your identity assets.

When I am speaking, I ask people in the audience what it says on their business cards. They all know. Their job title is ingrained in their consciousness like their names. They are the job, its embodiment. As they tell me their job titles, I can see the pride they take in the words. The word "Strategic" has a particular resonance. It makes people glow with pride. "Strategic Product Manager" has a ring which simple "Product Manager" fundamentally lacks.

I then ask people how close their job title is to what they do or of their talent potential? Does Strategic Product Manager say anything about a person's talent or the skills and intelligence they bring to the job? Of course not.

Job titles have, historically at least, been badges of status rather helpful descriptions of what people are good at.

So, six years ago I started to encourage my own colleagues to design their own business cards to visualize and label their knowledge navigation. They know who they are and what they are heading for.

It is happening. In the past couple of months I have bumped into a "detective of the future," "head of imagination" and come across a "choreographer" and the impressive "wow virus disseminator."

It's definitely spreading – *Fast Company* even has a regular section on new job titles. In May 2000 the Swedish Internet start-up company *wannago.com*, which handles entertainment and events, placed a full-page job recruitment ad for senior managers in the *Financial Times*. Among others it wanted to recruit a chief "making-the-customer-happy" officer, a "getting-the-numbers-in-order" officer and a chief "attracting-and-keeping-talent" officer. In the old economy, the ad explained, these would have been known as chief operating officer, finance VP and human resource manager.

The company went even further and pointed out in smaller print that people would be able to decide their own titles and even design their own business cards.

As well as spreading it's also going up and down the status ladder. Steve Jobs, founder of Apple Computers, now styles himself iCEO. Not to be outdone, Microsoft's Bill Gates may no longer be CEO or even iCEO but he is now "chief software architect" (and still old-fashioned chairman, of course).

And a recent survey in the UK revealed that 70 percent of office workers would be prepared to turn down more pay in return for a more dynamic title – "data storage specialist" rather than filing clerk, for example.

Lots of people believe that the whole idea of wacky labels began with Vermont hippy ice cream makers Ben and Jerry. The head flavor developer, after all, is called the "primal ice cream therapist" and one group of employees known as the Joy Gang is headed by the "grand Poobah of Joy." It will be interesting to see if the grand Poobah survives in the more staid Anglo-Dutch atmosphere of new owner Unilever.

Job titles might in some cases reflect a corporate culture. But more important is the shift to the emergent i-commerce, individuals visualizing their talent and trading on it. Instead of firms offering decades of employment, talent exchanges will emerge in which people move to and fro between organizations.

If you are going to take control of your knowledge, career and develop your identity assets, redefining your job is a starting point and a statement of intent. Most people are not allowed to shape their own business card or have their own web site. They have no mandate to be themselves. Create that mandate by beginning to experiment with your identity assets.

COMPASS LINKS
www.fastcompany.com
www.wizoz.co.uk

TAKING BEARINGS
- Who decides what goes on your business card?
- Is your current job title an accurate description of your talent?
- Do you have the mandate to change your business card?
- Do you have a personal web site?

Notes

1   This is also explored by Professor Bodil Jönsson, *Thoughtpower*, 2001.
2   Myhrvold, Nathan, "A revolution of the mind," *Fast Company*, September 2000
3   Barrett, Richard, "Liberating your soul," www.corptools.com
4   Professor Bengt Arnetz of the University of Uppsala is doing interesting work in this area. See www.ceos.nu
5   *Fast Company*, September 2000
6   "How much is enough," Christoph Niemann, *Fast Company*, July–August 1999
7   "Managing oneself," Peter F. Drucker, *Harvard Business Review*, March–April 1999
8   Strassmann, Paul, "Personal capitalists," *Knowledge Management*, May 2001
9   Cope, Mick, *Know Your Value*, Pearson Education, London, 2000

The Knowledge Innovation Dimension

The only vital value an enterprise has is the experience, skills, innovativeness and insights of its people.

INNOVATION PERSPECTIVES

What is it that triggers a spark of genius? Is there some encouragement given at the right time that starts the process or helps it along, or does genius simply find its expression despite all odds?

Young Albert Einstein was a quiet boy. "Perhaps too quiet," thought Hermann and Pauline Einstein. He spoke hardly at all until aged three. They might have thought him slow, but there was something else evident. When he did speak, he'd say the most unusual things. When Albert was two, Pauline promised him a surprise. Albert was elated, thinking she was bringing him some new fascinating toy. But when his mother presented him with his new baby sister Maja, all Albert could do was stare quizzically. Finally he responded, "where are the wheels?"

A couple of years later, Hermann Einstein brought the sick Albert a device that did stir his intellect. It was the first time he had seen a magnetic compass. He lay there shaking and twisting the odd contraption, certain he could fool it into pointing off in a new direction. But try as he might, the compass needle would always find its way back to pointing in the direction of magnetic north. "A wonder," he thought. The invisible force that guided the compass needle was evidence to Albert that there was more to our world that meets the eye. There was "something behind things, something deeply hidden."

So began Albert Einstein's journey down a road of exploration that he would follow the rest of his life. "I have no special gift," he would say, "I am only passionately curious."

His curiosity tugged at him constantly. He liked to wander the neighborhood, and his mother encouraged, rather than stifled, his explorations. Even as a young child he was allowed his freedom. He wasn't social and wasn't pushed to be so. He wasn't athletic, and that was okay too.

One advantage Albert Einstein's developing mind enjoyed was the opportunity to interact with adults in an intellectual way. His uncle, an engineer, would come to the house, and Albert would join in the discussions. His thinking was also stimulated by a medical student who came over once a week for dinner and lively banter.

Albert Einstein was more than just curious though. He had a patience and determination that kept him at things longer than most. He adopted mathematics as the tool he would use to pursue his curiosity and prove what he would discover about the behavior of the universe.

He was convinced that beauty lies in clarifying the simplistic. "When the solution is simple," he said, "God is answering." Perhaps this insight was the real empowerment of his genius. Albert Einstein looked for the beauty of simplicity in the apparent complexity of nature and saw truths that eluded others. While the expression of his mathematics might be accessible to only a few proficient in the science, Albert could condense the essence of his thoughts so anyone could understand.

We all now recognize that innovation matters and increasingly so. Organizations need to nurture their own Einsteins. "Every organization needs one core competence: innovation," says Peter Drucker. "Today the only way to have an advantage is through innovation," Harvard Business School luminary Michael Porter has observed. When one of the world authorities on global competitiveness, says so, CEOs tend to listen. Tom Peters is another outspoken advocate of innovation. "Top quality, reasonable price and good service

Organizations need to nurture their own Einsteins.

merely get you into the game; they're not enough to allow you to win. Innovate or die," says Peters with characteristic bluntness.

Look around. Walk through a shopping mall and reflect on how many of the retail names were there ten years ago. Look at the companies leading the Stock Exchange and reflect on the same question. *The Economist's* Innovation Survey noted that half of the growth in the American economy can be attributed to companies, which are less than ten years old. Companies have to innovate to stay alive. The paradox is that financial analysts still often make their forecasts on the strength of financial values over ten years. They need to move from business planning to strategies for innovation.[1]

Research confirms that innovation is now moving to the top of the boardroom agenda.[2] A PricewaterhouseCoopers survey of 800 board directors from companies across America, Europe, Australia and Japan shows that innovation is fast becoming the number one strategic issue for CEOs around the world.

The PwC findings, drawn from 26 sectors across seven countries, indicate "an inextricable link between innovation and value creation." Among the companies surveyed, a 10 percent increase in the proportion of turnover generated from products and services introduced in the last five years led to a 2.5 percent increase in revenue growth, year on year. Moreover, companies that generated 80 percent of their revenue from new products typically doubled their market capitalization over a five year period.

According to a further PwC report in August 2000, R&D's role is being broadened in technology companies thanks to new analytical tools and intensified emphasis on commercial innovation and speed to market. Its ivory tower past is being transformed into a future that is increasingly business and competitor focused. According to one of PwC's regular "Technology Barometer" surveys of US business, more than three in four business chiefs say integration of technology planning and business strategy influences their company's R&D efforts.

"The high importance accorded integration of technology planning and business strategy places R&D in the spotlight, at corporate center stage," says Paul Weaver, global technology industry leader for PwC. "Thanks to today's sophisticated information technology, R&D departments are gaining a faster, far better understanding of their science and the customer. This enables R&D to be more flexible, more adaptable to change. As a result, R&D is increasingly helping to grow revenues through creation of new products, processes, or services, and through the development of new markets. In so doing, it is building shareholder value and market share."

There is only one problem with all this: organizational systems are often not tuned into the pace of innovation. The market clock is ticking faster than the organizational watch. With a renewal speed of five percent it will take about 20 years to achieve renewal. Will the market context allow such a slow rate of renewal?

An outspoken and passionate champion of innovation, James Dyson, inventor of the eponymous Dyson Dual Cyclone vacuum cleaner, is not impressed by much of what he sees of innovation. "I have been developing new products for 30 years. Throughout this time, many people within manufacturing who should be introducing new products, remain remarkably unimaginative. They rely heavily on what their competitors are doing or what has sold in the past for new product ideas," observes Dyson. "It almost seems that knowledge of a competitor's products acts as a kind of anesthetic on that part of the brain which would normally stimulate them into finding out what people really want and what could sell in the future."

So how do you harness the potential of the innovation imperative? Opinions, inevitably, differ. I will present two major sources which seem to me to resonate with reality.

Debra Amidon, author of *Innovation Strategies for the Knowledge Economy* and founder of Entovation International suggests that "the real challenge facing most companies is that of faster innovation. Creating the system within which ideas are created and applied is more than management. It is a matter of strategy and leadership." She has developed the concept of Knowledge Innovation™ which she defines as "the creation, evolution, exchange and application of ideas for new products and services to benefit (1) the success of an enterprise (both profit and not for profit), (2) the vitality of a nation's economy, and (3) the advancement of society as a whole."

She says that there are four key concepts which make knowledge innovation unique:

- Innovation value system (not value chain) – value chain thinking is linear and static. The innovation value system is dynamic and shows all the interdependent relationships that need to be developed for successful innovation.
- Strategic business network (not strategic business units) – strategic business unit management tends to create isolated islands of knowledge. The strategic business network encourages the flow of knowledge between partners, customers, suppliers, research organizations and other stakeholders, including competitors, in the innovation process.
- Collaborative (not competitive) advantage – competitive strategies create win-lose scenarios, often competing for a share of the same pie. Collaborative strategies encourage

win-win situations through symbiotic relationships. Knowledge grows and the pie gets bigger for all.

- Customer success (not satisfaction) – customer satisfaction meets today's articulated need. A focus on the success of your customer helps identify those future unarticulated needs, the source of growth and future success.[3]

The second view is that of Baruch Lev. Lev points out that sustainability and survival – what the stock market appreciates – can only take place through investing in intangible innovation, that is, intellectual capital.

Lev has identified three basic parts to the process of innovation:

- **Discovery/learning** "In which new products (drugs, software, consumer electronics), processes (Internet-based supply or distribution channels) and services (risk management or internal control systems) are developed. These innovations are sometimes discovered internally by scientists and engineers (R&D), but increasingly are acquired from outside the organization. Learning from within (communities of practice) and from the outside (reverse engineering) plays an important role in the innovation process. The discovery/learning process is sometimes an outcome of a systematic strategy (e.g. the scientific approach to drug development), and other times the result of trial and error or sheer luck."

- **Implementation** "Achieving the stage of technological feasibility of products and services, such as drugs passing successfully phase III clinical tests, software products satisfying beta tests, or websites reaching a threshold number of unique visitors or repeat customers. Establishment of legally protected intellectual property rights, in the form of patents and trademarks often takes place during this phase."

- **Commercialization** "Technological feasibility is a necessary but not sufficient condition for economic success. Bringing new products/services quickly to the market and earning above-cost of capital return on the investment caps the innovation process ... The cellular phone technology was developed in the 1970s by AT&T yet while reaching technological feasibility AT&T abandoned the invention due to perceived lack of potential."[4]

As Debra and Baruch's insights suggest, the starting point must be to harness new innovative perspectives. Innovation requires that you seek out new perspectives – on everything. IC becomes I see.

Innovative companies are always trying out different ways of doing things, through rapid prototyping. As Leonardo da Vinci said, we need at least three perspectives on every question or problem.

Ben & Jerry's Home-made Ice Cream, for example, is famous for its innovative flavors – and creative names. Successes include Cherry Garcia, after the late Grateful Dead guitarist Jerry Garcia, Chubby Hubby and Chunky Monkey. But coming up with new ideas year after year isn't easy. To stay fresh, the company instituted "Dessert Tours." Employees from R&D go on annual culinary tours of leading American restaurants on the East and West coast, chatting to top chefs and customers to get insights from the leading edge of food. They ask what flavors and ingredients are popular this season, and could be big in the ice cream world.

> **Innovation requires that you seek out new perspectives – on everything.**

Stimulus can come from almost anything which jolts thinking and creates new alternatives, anything from meetings with strangers to magazine articles or movies.

At Van den Berghs, a food subsidiary of Unilever, people are encouraged to get out of the office and seek relevant stimulus which they can then relate back to the project they are working on. Whole cupboards of stuff are collected and used throughout a product development project. Accounting staff even ventured out from the company's offices at Crawley in the UK to nearby Gatwick Airport in search of stimulus for more imaginative ways of presenting financial information.

While the vast majority of companies continue to focus on beating their rivals, the best strategies are those that break free from the traditional knowledge cluster and create what Chan Kim and Renee Mauborgne of INSEAD call "new market space". In other words, going toe-to-toe with your main rivals and slugging it out in the arena of the established market is short-sighted. It results in incremental improvements in performance – in cost, quality or both – which give only a temporary advantage as rivals quickly catch up.

Innovative companies have a different approach. They look outside business sectors to identify unoccupied market space. In this way they create products or services for which there are no direct competitors. They add value in this way. They look upon the future as an asset to be addressed, navigated towards and cultivated. The traditional approach is a firm built around maintenance, in which investing in the future is cost accounted as a liability. The future demands a new outlook. It is only through seeking out new perspectives that we can gain fresh insights. If you see the same things you will always think the same things.

COMPASS LINKS
www.entovation.com
www.baruch-lev.com
www.gslis.utexas.edu/darius

TAKING BEARINGS
- How do you encourage curiosity and knowledge innovation?
- How much do you invest in the future as a percentage of your time?
- What indicators and stories about innovation do you tell?

INNOVATION SPACE

The second important ingredient for innovation is space. This is white space management, managing the space between the organizational boxes. People need space to innovate, the freedom to explore. They need to be able to make mistakes. "Knowledge can only be volunteered; it cannot be conscripted," observes David Snowden of IBM's Institute of Knowledge Management. To volunteer knowledge, people need an environment that encourages a degree of risk-taking. By definition, that means being more tolerant of failure. But as they grow larger many lose this.

"I invented a thousand ways not to invent the light bulb before I invented the light bulb," Thomas Edison once observed. The trouble is that in traditional companies, he would have either been fired or the project cancelled long before he got it right.

Ideas need space to grow. People who are good at innovating are open-minded enough to think ideas through to explore their potential. That means suspending judgement and resisting the urge to do instant analysis. Some companies have developed their own structures to support this. For example, Southwest Airlines is an official "no zinger" zone. Zingers, in Southwest parlance, are "undermining critical/judgmental comments." So strongly does the company value new ideas that repeat offenders can be fired for their crimes against the company culture.

Give people time and you don't know what will emerge. 3M did just that with its 15 percent policy. What freedom from the corporate yoke. The 15 percent policy is called, among other things, "the bootleg policy" – it may also be called a competitive advantage because it has helped foster and nurture so many good ideas (most notably the Post-it).

The 15 percent policy encourages researchers to roam further afield.

"The object is to spur as many ideas as possible because perhaps 1 in 1000 will turn out to fit," explains Post-it developer, Art Fry. "An idea might be a perfectly good idea for another company, but not for yours. Putting together a new product is like putting together a jigsaw puzzle such as raw material suppliers, distributors, government regulations, and the amount of capital you have to spend. If one part doesn't fit, the whole project can fail. Your work might have been brilliant but somebody else dropping the ball can lead to failure."

The London-based consultancy ?What If! is regarded as a leader in the emerging field of creativity training and culture change. According to co-founder Matt Kingdon: "If you ask senior managers, they all say innovation is important. But most companies don't really understand how it works and how to make people more creative. The problem in many big companies is that there's not enough scope to try out new ideas. There's no room for experimentation."

When Dave Allan and Matt Kingdon left their marketing jobs at Unilever to set up their own business in 1992 they had one simple goal: to create the best innovation company in the world. From experience, they knew they had their best ideas away from the office.

So they turned the office into a home from home, complete with rugs, armchairs and a table football game. They hold client meetings in the kitchen and even run a company slate at the local pub. Such eccentric behavior may sound more like student high jinx than a serious business, but at ?What If! they are hardened marketing professionals who have grown a multi-million dollar business from harnessing the power of human imagination.

They recognized the need to help free the imagination and encourage innovation in all companies. They were joined by Kristina Murrin, a former brand manager at Procter & Gamble and Daz Rudkin, another ex-Unilever marketing manager.

They describe the management style as the "serious relaxed business"– something that seems to appeal to big corporates. Today, in most economically slimmed organizations there's no room for experimentation or invention.

"Have fun to encourage fun" is also part of the management philosophy. As well as a profit share scheme, the company subscribes to the "James Brown Principle" – a range of initiatives designed to make staff "feel good." These include paid for visits to the office from a yoga teacher; deliveries of fresh fruit; and company accounts at local pubs – where employees go on a Friday night.

The most important rule is to break the rules.

Or look at creative juices allowed to flow at IDEO. *Fortune* magazine once described the company's seemingly chaotic design studio as "one of Silicon Valley's secret weapons." It is an environment which has spawned such diverse projects as helping create the very first Apple Computer mouse and the design of the 25-foot mechanical whale in the *Free Willy* films.

Despite intense pressure and tight deadlines, the company maintains an air of creative anarchy, which it believes is the ultimate innovation environment. It is a kind of chaordic model. Staff are encouraged to "play" at work, and the most important rule is to break the rules. (Play is a recurring theme among organizations which succeed in sharing knowledge. "Creating bulletproof products and defensible strategic positions is yesterday's game. Today you need the ability and willpower to constantly develop and deploy new products that respond to changing customer needs. It requires an organization with the flexibility and competitive energy of a kid playing a video game rather than the analytical consistency of a grand master trying to hang on in a three-day chess match," says Skandia's Jan R. Carendi, who was one of my key mentors when starting the Skandia Future Center.[5])

Along with the last word in computer imaging, IDEO offices are literally strewn with cardboard, foam, wood and plastic prototypes. Staff work wherever they happen to be and scribbled notes are scattered all around. To the untrained eye it may look like a chaotic mess. But David Kelley, the company's founder and front man, describes the firm as "a living laboratory of the workplace." "The company is in a state of perpetual experimentation," he said. "We're constantly trying new ideas in our projects, our work space, even our culture."

But it is the company's special approach to brainstorming which has attracted the attention of other firms. These sessions have been elevated almost to the status of a science. Typically, project leaders call a brainstorming session at the start of a new assignment. People are invited to attend, and most sessions involve a multi-disciplinary group of around eight participants. (Attendance is voluntary, but refusal to take part is frowned upon.)

Once the brainstorming starts, participants can doodle or scribble on almost anything – there are whiteboards on the walls, and conference tables are covered in white paper. Low tech is accompanied by high-tech in the form of multimedia presentations using video and computer projections.

To ensure the best results, the firm's five principles of brainstorming are displayed on the walls:

- Stay focused on the topic;
- Encourage wild ideas;
- Defer judgement;
- Build on the ideas of others;
- One conversation at a time.

The aim is to create a whirlwind of activity and ideas. Speed is essential to the process, with the most promising ideas being developed and worked up into prototypes in just a few days. To make brain storming more effective, the company has also developed a special type of camera copier which photographs whatever drawing and scribblings emerge from the sessions.

IDEO's brainstorming plainly works. There is nothing brilliantly original about it - and therein lies the attraction. Indeed, I worked with Gordon Edge at PA's Technology Centre in Cambridge on brainstorming activities for new business development 25 years ago.

Companies that excel at innovation accept its inherent messiness. They cut people some slack. Microsoft and Apple are both famous for hiring smart people and giving them some elbowroom. The companies run perpetual pilots. They try out ideas no matter what. They let people run free.

COMPASS LINKS
www.ideo.com
www.changeisfun.com

TAKING BEARINGS
- How much freedom do you have to pursue experimental projects?
- How does brain stilling work in your organization?
- Where in the organizational chart do you find the act of innovation?
- How is failure treated in your organization?

INNOVATING CULTURE

Innovation is also a matter of culture. Organizations that are consistently in the vanguard are those that have successfully fostered an innovation culture. Enter IDEO and you can sense the company's outlook and attitude within seconds.

"The main reason that organizations are unable to mine the creative potential of their employees is that they fail to understand the importance of linking the well-being and survival of their employees to the well-being and survival of the company. When the link between effort and reward is severed, and you are paid to do, rather than think, there is no incentive to achieve optimal performance. It is only when people feel a direct link between their own contribution, the success of the company and their personal reward that they assume responsibility for the whole. When this happens they feel encouraged to fulfil their potential," says Richard Barrett former values co-ordinator at the World Bank.[6]

The pharmaceuticals giant Pfizer has an impressive track record in this field. The company says it's important to realize that innovation doesn't begin and end with R&D. "We need to recognize that innovation isn't just about sexy products. It's a way of life and an attitude. It's about the way administrative staff think about internal processes, and all the other aspects of the business," says Simon Norris, HR director of Pfizer's operating division. R&D is just one dimension of Pfizer's innovation culture that extends to marketing, manufacturing and support functions.

"We try to keep the paraphernalia simple," says Pfizer's Simon Norris. "Rather than putting layer after layer like wallpaper on a wall, you have to create a connected system. If you have a values statement that includes innovation, as we do, then that is translated into behaviors. We have role profiles which set out the behaviors expected. This is then directly supported by appraisals, which include not just the hard targets but the soft ones as well – how people behave."

One of the most effective ways to support innovation is to put structures in place which underpin the new culture. A structure is any process, mechanism or device that simplifies creative behavior. These can be used to reinforce the adoption of new behaviors; the acquisition of new skills; and a nurturing environment.

For example, Walt Disney's famous imagineers, the team of developers that design Disney theme parks, has designated names for different types of meetings. Open Forums allow any member of staff to present a new idea to senior management – they have five minutes to set up and five minutes to present.

"If you can't put the idea over in five minutes, then you don't know the concept well enough," says Mike West, senior show producer. Then there are Charettes – brainstorming sessions when the team needs to come up with an idea quickly.

Consider the Unilever subsidiary Van den Berghs. Marketing director John Coombs explains the logic behind its work on creating an innovation-driven culture: "We were a very conservative company. A company of this size has to have planning systems in place. But those inevitable levels of bureaucracy can stifle creativity, fleetness of foot, and time to market."

Senior management recognized that an innovation culture required their active commitment. "The danger was that over time our products wouldn't be sufficiently exciting," says Coombs. "You have to take a leap of faith sometimes."

In 1998, Van den Bergh took the creative plunge. A "drive team" was set up, with representatives from senior management. The aim was to make innovation a business priority. The marketing function, for example, linked innovation directly to the business strategy. This included demanding stretch targets (dubbed "tough love"). New creative behaviors were also made explicit.

Where culture and the need for new perspectives come together is in the growing acceptance that innovation is a matter of sharing perspectives. Organizations and individuals must be open to sharing and working within cultures geared towards trust and sharing. Remember the organizational models we explored earlier? Chaordic alliances and networked incubators are concerned with sharing experiences, ideas, passing ideas to and fro, and, of course, sharing the risk. In Skandia Jan Carendi called this a High Trust Culture (HTC).

Seeking new perspectives often means working with other organizations.

Seeking new perspectives often means working with other organizations. "Knowledge can only be generated in highly collaborative relationships," says Hubert Saint-Onge of Clarica. He has, therefore, replaced the HR function with a membership and partnership function.

Pfizer has created new market opportunities through collaborations with smaller pharmaceutical companies. Since 1997, for example, the company has co-marketed Lipitor™ – a leading product for reducing blood cholesterol – with the Warner Lambert group. It also co-markets a drug to combat Alzheimer's disease with the Japanese company Eisai.

In its industry, Pfizer has deliberately positioned itself as the "co-marketer of choice" – underlining the point that a true innovation culture can create new opportunities in a variety of ways.

Sharing means looking beyond what is normal, and expected. Management consultants Chuck Lucier and Janet Torsilieri point out that the route to greater innovation is universally accepted: be better, faster, and do it more often and more efficiently.[7] This works. But it relies on internal resources. They suggest that "unbundling innovation by leveraging the talents of superstars who are not employees" can lead to more dramatic changes in performance. Look beyond the R&D department and you may reap incredible benefits.

Lucier and Torsilieri suggest the entertainment industry as a role model. Entertainment is characterized by a reliance on a small number of "blockbuster products" and an equally small number of superstars who have a track record of success. The talented individuals can operate as individual brands and move around between companies and projects (described earlier as i-commerce). Increasingly these superstars share the risks on the projects they work on.

The secret, therefore, is to combine a superstar talent with "increased scope." The latter is defined as "the number of people who benefit from his or her talent." Michael Jordan could earn far more than Babe Ruth because 160 million people watched the 1998 basketball play-offs, more than witnessed Babe Ruth's entire career.

The rise of superstar economics presents companies with a number of pointed and difficult questions. These include: "How can you best gain access to tomorrow's superstar innovators? What is the best combination of strategies – process improvements, best practice sharing and using superstars – to become more innovative? How can you drive increases in the scope of your best products and brands?" The future lies in the hands of the talented innovator, a new type of intellectual entrepreneurship. Talent will be all.

Another cultural approach is to outsource innovation. James Brian Quinn of Dartmouth College's Tuck Business School, says that no one company can hope to innovate purely in-house, especially in such high-tech sectors as biotechnology and pharmaceuticals. Far better, argues Quinn, to outsource R&D to small specialized, nimble companies.[8] And, adds Quinn, it can lessen a new danger – that of a company becoming "obsolete" through not participating in outside innovation.

There are just too many brains in the world for companies to be comfortable about doing all their innovation in-house, according to Quinn. Four forces are driving this "innovation revolution": demand is doubling every 14 to 16 years, creating new specialist markets attractive to innovation; the supply of qualified knowledge workers and knowledge bases is skyrocketing; the ability to cooperate has grown; and incentives such as lower tax rates and privatization around the world have given entrepreneurs the incentive to develop and exploit advances in knowledge.

Successful outsourcing of innovation involves scanning for the best opportunities, much as a surfer scans the ocean for the best waves. Since there are many such waves in today's turbulent markets, the trick is to use experience to assess where the best are likely to occur, position the company accordingly, and then ride them quickly when they arrive. Are you ready to grab the wave? Or, as Gary Hamel of Strategos puts it: Do you have an approach to find the right combination of genes, innovation genes inside and outside?

COMPASS LINKS
www.strategosnet.com

TAKING BEARINGS
- How many pilots of intellectual entrepreneurship are now up and running in your organization?
- What does the innovational organizational gene look like?
- How does your community insource and outsource its i-processes?

WELCOME ABOARD

Put all these aspects of innovation together and you may emerge with something similar to the concept of Futureship Øresund, which is envisaged as Denmark's Future Center. Enter its ship-like base and you are greeted by the smell of cinnamon buns on your way to the IC-community club, oasis, café. This spacious room is the deck of a ship decorated with green plants under an enormous white sail. There are great glass walls towards the open deck where there are comfortable deck chairs. In the far corner there are the flames of the open grill and here you are welcome to join in the cooking if you feel like it. You can help yourself to food and drink from the buffet whenever you feel like it.

Then there is the "stairway to heaven," a staircase which extends towards a platform where you can enjoy the spectacular view. The "stairway to heaven" also acts as a theater – a place where nearly 400 people can participate in events.

Among the activities at the Center are knowledge safaris with expedition leaders. All interior furnishings materials are ergonomic and comfortable. The shapes are rounded as circles and spirals are also symbols of the cyclical process of learning.

Under a giant sail people can check in for a day's work or for as long as they wish. There are no cell offices or mahogany desks. The emphasis is on exchanging knowledge in a social community. People work together, as a competence alliance, a network of individuals/units/companies with various competence profiles. This is virtual enterprising, people coming together in an arena rather than an office to explore their collective talent potential.

Overhead a big screen shows what is going on at the Center alternating with product spots and inspiring pictures. The Center plans to be open to the public at weekends. The great theater is used for performances, artists can come and work in the studio light at "community square" and the foyer functions as a gallery.

Under its "Captain" Mette Laursen and "Protector" Lars Kolind, the path breaking former Oticon CEO, the vision of the Future Center Danmark is to create an arena for innovation, development and the growth of intellectual capital within society, companies, organizations and

Circles and spirals are also symbols of the cyclical process of learning.

individuals. The Center is planned to be built as an extraordinary ship, but the most extraordinary element is the new organizational concept it represents. "The knowledge-based corporation is not only a vision. For me, it's been a reality," says Kolind.

The business concept is a "solution alliance" in which companies come together not as a characterless holding company but a customer-oriented alliance where foresight and results are the bottom-line.

The partners provide financial capital and will be deeply involved and co-branded in the development of the concept.

Member companies – called "citizens" – will pay a yearly fee to access the Center's facilities. They have access to the ship and to a range of the facilities, prototyping projects and happenings.

One of the core elements of the Center's activities is IC Prototyping in which several participating organizations work together to develop a prototype. The partners and citizens provide their own resources and organization for developing and visualizing the IC-prototypes as well as using collective workspaces, knowledge expeditions and the like in relation to the projects at the Center.

The future is here.

Some may not wish to set sail on such an imagination-laden craft. They may prefer the less wacky but equally innovative reincarnation of my former colleague Sir Gordon Edge. Gordon's office is now in a renovated eighteenth century mill house, in rural Cambridgeshire. Harston Mill is the headquarters of the Generics Group of which Edge is the founder and CEO.

Generics is a hybrid: part scientific research company, part technology consulting firm, and part incubator. It funds research in optics, new materials, and telecoms, licensing its IPR to other companies, many of them in the U.S. Generics is listed on the Stock Exchange in London and has IKEA as one of its largest shareholders.

Relative competitive advantage is derived from the skills of the people.

"Generics is my third business. Each has been built on legacy code from the previous. With Generics, I really tried to understand and optimize the management theory around the way people behave and are motivated – to optimize creativity," says Gordon Edge.

To address this issue he developed a model called skill-based competition. "Most management theories tend to be superficial. I tried to get evidence to support my model. I found there is a strong link with technology companies between added value and skills intensity. This suggests that relative competitive advantage is derived from the skills of the people."

Edge's insight was that the value added in high tech is driven by the earlier mentioned SQ dimension. The original Generics business plan sought to optimize that model. It is a simple model.

Stage 1

Addresses the basic needs of a business to generate cash. This requires a consulting business. Working closely with *Fortune 500* and *Times 100* companies, helping them solve their issues, established a creative environment and culture. It fosters creative turmoil. The business plan started with the consulting business. This generated the cash to invest in the next phase.

Stage 2

Involved building specialized laboratories for rapid prototyping and investing in R&D.

Stage 3

Out of this comes the incubation of new enterprising, which can then be spun-off. In this sense, Generics is a microcosm of what happens in Cambridge. It's a hotbed of people who are able to take controlled risks and develop emerging technology to create new businesses rooted in science.

Stage 4

The fourth part is putting money into new technology companies. This involves the creation of an investment company which invests in incubating fledgling businesses within Generics, but also other people's businesses. "We are a very early stage investor," says Edge. "We often get involved long before a VC will put money into a technology. Often we are the only investor."

The Generics business model today is the same as it was in 1986 when the company started. All that's changed in the intervening years is the scale of the operation.

"It's actually quite a difficult model to operate because it's capital intensive. You have to build the labs first. Then you have to create the right environment that optimizes that and rewards people for staying with the company," says Gordon Edge.

To this simple model, Generics has brought into play some of the motivational factors. "We set out to create a challenging environment – I mean intellectually challenging. We use a peer group process of review. Typically this involves groups of 10 people, who are experts in a field, challenging an individual's assumptions. This is common in academia but not in the business context."

All Generics staff are encouraged to present their ideas to the company's Innovation Exploitation Board (IEB), which provides funding to support commercially the best technologies emerging from Generics. Employees who win funds also receive the time and business support necessary to incubate their ideas until they are ready to be exploited commercially.

The age of innovation truly is the space age, an age which requires experiments with new vessels as well as 3D knowledge navigation.

COMPASS LINKS
www.futurecenter.dk
www.generics.com

TAKING BEARINGS
- How does your organization prototype new ideas?
- How many alliances is you organization involved in?
- How do you learn and work with people from other organizations?

Notes

1 This is spelled out by David Mahdjoubi of the University of Texas.
2 "Innovation and Growth: A Global Perspective," Dec 1999, PricewaterhouseCoopers
3 www.entovation.com/innovation/knowinno.htm Dr Amidon is now working on her next book *The Innovation SuperHighway – Challenge of the Third Millennium*.
4 Lev, Baruch, "New accounting for the new economy," May 2000
5 Ghoshal, Sumantra, & Bartlett, Christopher, "Beyond strategic planning to organizational learning," *Strategy & Leadership*, Jan/Feb 1998

6 Barrett, Richard, "Liberating your soul," www.corptools.com
7 Lucier, Charles, and Torsilieri, Janet, "To win with innovation – kill R&D," *Strategy & Business*, Third Quarter 1999
8 "Outsourcing Innovation: the new engine of growth," James Brian Quinn, *Sloan Management Review*, Summer 2000

Leading with a Compass

The leader always required a compass. Now the leader must possess a mental compass.

LEADING THE NEW GENERATION

Today, the leader's role has never been so demanding; nor share-holders so unforgiving. The list of derailed leaders grows longer by the day. In February 2001 alone, no fewer than 119 CEOs left significant US companies. In all, more than 1,000 US CEOs walked the plank in the previous year. Two-thirds of all major companies worldwide have replaced their CEO at least once since 1995.

Failure is becoming endemic.

Those at the top are feeling the pressure. At the 2001 Davos summit, Dan Vasella, CEO of Novartis, acknowledged that he was "sometimes overwhelmed" by his job. Former Toshiba CEO Taizo Nishimura admitted: "I enjoyed being a CEO but I confess now I feel free and relaxed, having retired."

What we are witnessing is a confluence of factors that make the job more difficult than ever before:

Complexity

First, there is the undoubted issue of complexity. Complexity is not just a theory; for leaders it is a fact of life. "The job is more complex," agrees Warren Bennis of the University of Southern California and an acknowledged expert on business leaders, "a more clogged cartography of stakeholders, unbelievable changes, disruptive technologies, globalization, inflection points no one would even think about 10 years ago and most of all, speed. It not only takes a strong stomach and a tough nervous system but a mind that can take nine points of view and connect the dots."

Great expectations

Expectations add to the burden. There are contradictory pressures. Leaders are routinely expected to make quick decisions while keeping a long-term perspective; and to reconcile the imperative for performance with ethical concerns and questions of corporate responsibility. Leaders are pilloried for dishonesty but stock prices collapse when they are honest. It's a juggling act that very few people can pull off for long.

Impossible workloads

With complexity comes an increasing workload. The modern corporate leader has a daunting panoply of roles and constituencies to contend with. The role is increasingly fragmented. There is little time to do everything well and so the leader faces a continuing series of trade-offs of time, energy and focus. Brain stress is fact of life for the modern leader.

Media scrutiny

Leaders are under the spotlight as never before. Their work and lives are examined from every angle. Every decision, word, and gesture is pored over by financial analysts, business academics and the media. Increasingly, too, leaders are being scrutinized by those outside the business community: non-government organizations, including environmental and other pressure groups; politicians; and consumers now take a growing interest.

The end result is that some leaders are adrift, floating helplessly. "Things are so complex and happening so fast that most CEOs are feeling overwhelmed," says top CEO-coach Robert "Dusty" Staub, author of *The 7 Acts of Courage* and co-author of *The Heart of Leadership.* "Expectations are now outrageous. They suffer from hollow man syndrome. They know they don't know it all, but are still expected to know it all." Little wonder that the wisdom of going for the top jobs is now being questioned. "In some firms people are already turning down the top jobs," says Robin Linnecar, director of the leadership development company Whitehead Mann The Change Partnership. "It is not an epidemic but people are questioning whether it's worth it."

And then the final twist: In addition to these factors, leaders now have to lead a generation whose values are very different. They are increasingly leading a generation that don't want to be led in the same ways. Indeed, some do not want to be led at all.

The generation posing these leadership questions is the first generation of young people to grow up with the Internet who are now entering the workforce. These teenagers and early twentysomethings have been called variously the Net Generation, Gen e, Millenniums, Generation www, and the first wave of Generation Y.

Their agendas are different and issue a challenge to traditional leadership. "First of all, the work/life balance is a very big issue for them," says Jay Conger of London Business School. "They want greater flexibility around work times for example. So companies need to be much more open to different start times and end of day times. Second, they do not want jobs that consume them. This is a product of the dual career lives of their parents. They saw how little time their parents often had for them. They also saw careers derail marriages."

This is supported by a survey of 350 final year Oxford University students. The survey sought to understand what motivates young people to join established firms. It found that the most valued factors were ranked as balance between work and leisure; pay; foreign travel; pension; private healthcare; gym membership; and, lastly, a car. "Young people have a very different attitude to work. They have very high self esteem, are much less hierarchical and will not tolerate old style command and control structures," says Alex Cheatle, managing director of tenUK, which commissioned the research. Similar studies are also performed by the Swedish research firm Universum and published as a Youth Barometer.

It may be youthful idealism, but money appears to be less important to the net generation. What is more likely to motivate is a "cool" work environment and a strong sense of community. "They want work places that have a community-like feeling," says Conger. "So you will see many newer companies with open work spaces, more community work spaces, community kitchens where the refrigerators are stocked with free cokes, sodas, desserts, snacks."

Then there is the greying dimensions of demography. The intriguing challenge of leadership is the combination of crossing age, cultural and geographical barriers. The result of all these factors is that our traditional notions of leadership are being questioned. Harvard Business School's John Kao suggests that three basic skills are now needed – the abilities to clear the mind, clear the place and clear the beliefs. This, he says, requires a new managerial mindset.[1]

Some insights to the nature of this mindset are offered by a survey of the most admired knowledge leaders carried out by Teleos and Work Frontiers International.[2] The criteria decided on for this award were that a leader must:

- consistently provide vision, strategic direction and leadership to the enterprise,
- be ultimately accountable for the success of the enterprise by meeting or surpassing both financial and non-financial strategic enterprise goals or operational performance targets,
- serve as the primary executive sponsor, champion, or, spokesperson for knowledge efforts within the enterprise.

As Arian Ward, president and CEO of Work Frontiers observes: "Behind every highly successful knowledge-based enterprise today is a leader with the wisdom to sense what the enterprise needs to be to thrive in the new economy, the ability to inspire everyone in the enterprise to co-create a shared vision of what that means to them, and the unwavering commitment to do whatever it takes to evolve and make that shared vision a reality – no matter what the obstacles or how long it takes. These knowledge leaders understand at a deep level what it means to be a 'knowledge-based enterprise' and can clearly articulate, model and motivate the mindset and behaviors that drive this culture of collective innovation, knowledge sharing and learning."

COMPASS LINKS

www.lbs.ac.uk
www.knowledgebusiness.com
www.workfrontiers.com
www.universum.se
www.entovation.com/kleadmap/index.htm
www.entovation.com/momentum/globalmn.htm
www.entovation.com/momentum/entovation-100.htm

TAKING BEARINGS

- How do you nourish the balance between leadership and life?
- How do you make sure that you are in touch with the net generation as well as other generations?
- How do you cultivate your leadership compass?

REFINING NAVIGATIONAL LEADERSHIP

For the time being, the reinvention of leadership, the emergence of the new managerial mindset, is notable for its general absence. New thinking on leadership remains largely theoretical.

Most notably, for all the work on leadership and the hefty weight of research, we remain wedded to the idea of heroic leadership. In the business world, the mythologizing of the CEO began in earnest about 20 years ago, with the lionization of Lee Iacocca, whose Herculean turnaround of Chrysler made him the idol of corporate America. In the 1990s, the techno-savant CEO moved center stage with the likes of Bill Gates, John Chambers, and Michael Dell. But it is Jack Welch at GE who has come to epitomize the CEO as maximum leader – a human dynamo who can transform any company, no matter how big or complicated, into an engine of perpetual over-performance. "It's a persistent myth in our culture that a single individual leads and other individuals follow," observes Stephen Denning.[3]

The heroic leader creates order. They show us where we need to go and then lead us in that direction. They are dictators, creators of certainty.

The trouble with this is twofold. First, as we have seen, people no longer respond to such a dictatorial style of leadership. Neither the net generation nor the seniors generation can be managed dictatorially.

Secondly, certainties are often an illusion. Nothing is neat any more. Indeed, Tom Peters argues that leadership is no longer a question of creating order, but of creating stimulatingly chaotic environment, a productive mess. His message is that leadership is no longer a simplistic matter of creating a vision and galvanizing the troops into action. The troops aren't easily convinced. Leadership, says Peters, is "confusing as hell" – "if we're going to make any headway in figuring out the new rules of leadership, we might as well say it up front: There is no one-size-fits-all approach to leadership. Leadership mantra #1: It all depends." Improvisation seems as important as traditional business planning.

Today's leaders operate in an entirely new environment. If they are to operate successfully they will have to refine their behavior and attitude.

In many ways leadership styles must begin to mirror the flexible, more freeflowing structures I described earlier. Chaordic organizations require chaordic leaders. Leading in one of the emergent organizational structures is a great deal different from leading a neatly hierarchical organization in which everyone knows their place and does what they are told.

Bill Critchley, business director of Ashridge Consulting, is researching what happens to new CEOs. "What we're finding supports the emerging view of organizations as complex social processes, rather than machines. This view suggests that organizations are inherently unpredictable. This challenges the conventional view, which was based on a cybernetic approach to organizations that has dominated since Frederick Taylor. It was an engineering view that suggested they could be controlled like a heating system.

"But as the world becomes more complex, as communication increases exponentially, the view that the CEO can control the organization unravels. There used to be a view that you could set a five year strategy and prescribe behavior to get there. Now we know that it doesn't work like that. If this organizational model is flawed then leaders have to give up trying to control **Chaordic organizations require chaordic leaders.** people. They need to create the conditions to help people deal with the inherent uncertainty, and to be innovative in their responses."

Leadership is no longer a matter of individualism. "Successful CEOs simply lead, or better, they make sure a leadership climate is fostered and maintained. They succeed by sharing leadership. They no longer command; they coach. The special duty of the CEO is to ensure that a climate of leadership exists everywhere in the organization. The modern CEO inspires," says Laurence Lyons, senior vice-president of the Executive Coaching Network. "In practice the CEO often excels simply by doing the things that no-one else in the company would ever think of doing."

Heroic leadership was one-dimensional. Now leaders must lead in three dimensions. There is more to it than that. Bruce A. Pasternack, Thomas D. Williams and Paul F. Anderson, all consultants with Booz-Allen & Hamilton, argue that there is now a move towards institutionalizing leadership.[4] They claim that leadership need not be a solo act by a charismatic leader. Rather, leadership can be a strategic asset whose strength is measured as the institution's Leadership Quotient, or LQ. The sourcing of LQ will then become a strategic indicator and part of the annual IC report.

Their research was based on surveys and interviews conducted for the World Economic Forum's Strategic Leadership Project and Booz-Allen. Surveys were completed by more than 4,000 leaders and managers at all levels in a dozen large organizations on three continents and 20 to 40 individuals in each of these companies was interviewed.

It revealed that companies are now creating systems that enable leadership to flourish up and down their ranks. LQ, they say, can be developed, nurtured, and increased through appropriate effort.

The down-top leadership required in the knowledge economy is called "grassroots leadership" at Royal/Dutch Shell. This addition to the management vocabulary is attributed to Steve Miller, group managing director of Shell. Miller observed the difficulties the company was experiencing in becoming more creative, innovative and faster moving. It was attempting to transform itself one layer of management at a time. Change quickly became becalmed.

The argument is logical. Solo leadership in the corporate world is ultimately inefficient and ineffective. No one individual, no matter how gifted, can be right all the time; no one individual, particularly in a large organization, has the relevant information to make every important decision. Over time, resources become misallocated, opportunities are missed, innovation becomes stifled. Over-control saps initiative and bureaucratic behavior ensues.

Some companies, say Pasternack, Williams and Anderson, and some business units within others, are characterized by a different pattern of leadership. Key tasks and responsibilities of leadership are institutionalized in the systems, practices, and cultures of the organization. At Skandia, we shaped a function for IC with an intellectual capital director (defined as a senior management position with responsibility for the company's utilization and development of intellectual capital). Or it can be a role like director of strategic capabilities taken by Hubert St Onge at Clarica.

In high-LQ organizations, many people act more like owners and entrepreneurs than employees and hired hands. They assume owner-like responsibility for financial performance and management of risk and they take initiatives to solve problems and, in general, act with a sense of urgency.

When high-LQ companies succeed, they develop the institutional equivalent of great individual leadership. The good fortune of having a Jack Welch at the helm is as rare as it is desirable. However, high-LQ companies get many of the benefits of such leadership without a superstar in the executive suite. Strong systems can also offset the morale-sapping effects of arbitrary, erratic, indecisive, weak, or egotistic leadership.

Moving beyond the heroic leader requires a major change, one summed up by Richard Barrett, former values coordinator at the World Bank: "Corporate transformation is about personal transformation. It is about the willingness of the leadership to shift its philosophy from what's in it for me to what's best for the common good."[5]

COMPASS LINKS
www.bah.com
www.chaordica.com
www.workfrontiers.com

TAKING BEARINGS
- How inclusive is your leadership style?
- Who do you think of when you think of a great leader?
- How would you describe your leadership style in terms of LQ?

SHAPING LEADERSHIP PERSPECTIVES

The new perspective of the leader is as a subtle and sensitive navigator of volunteers.

The human and humane side of leadership has never been more important. The new source of competitive advantage, says Sumantra Ghoshal, is "dreams and ambitions. Today we are in the world of the volunteer employee. People choose to invest their human capital in companies to get the best returns. They are mobile investors." Skandia AFS was actually labeled by Jan R. Carendi an organization of volunteers.

Leaders have, therefore, to be persuaders rather than dictators. "Many people tell me what I ought to do and just how I ought to do it, but few have made me want to do something," observed Mary Parker Follett early in the last century.[6]

Curt Carlson, CEO and president of SRI International says: "CEOs have always done many of the things I do today. But the difference now is that people can walk out the door. A dictatorial CEO is bad business. Good business is about engaging with the people. Getting agreement on the fundamental goals and values is a long process. None of these things are about CEO edicts. I don't have the knowledge to do that. The real knowledge resides in our people. You have to tap into their genius and potential."

Another view comes from Gurnek Bains, managing director of the business psychology consultancy, YSC: "CEOs often fail not because of lack of strategic thinking but a lack of coherent thought about implementation and mobilizing the organization. It really is about people. Before being CEOs managers usually understand this intellectually, but only when they actually do the job do they tend to understand it emotionally. Typically CEOs spend 40 to 50 percent of their time communicating with people. They also spend a surprising amount of time thinking about the top talent in the company, building teams and attracting talented people."

The new perspective of the leader is to take people out of their comfort zone.

"I don't think the job is impossible. CEOs just need to be more thoughtful. They need to step back and think about the nature of their business. If they do that then I think the job is doable. I actually think it's a great time to be a CEO. Sure, there are some irrational demands placed on them, but they need to think their way through that," says James Champy, the re-engineering guru whose intellectual focus has now shifted to the universal truths of ambition. "When we read about so and so who has been brought in as CEO we read about their stock options and the companies current plight. There's very little written about their ambitions. When the CEO tries to explain his or her vision to their people in the company, it tends to be too broad – which makes it weak. It's very seldom personal to them. If you expose your personal ambitions you are much more likely to engage people than talking about vision. But CEOs are uncomfortable about that. They are fearful of making themselves vulnerable. I believe truly great managers are prepared to make themselves vulnerable. But this means they could be wrong."

Vulnerability was never on the leader's traditional agenda. But why not? Leaders who operate in an emotional and commercial comfort zone are unlikely to make the next great leap forwards into knowledge economics. Indeed, they are unlikely to do much of anything.

The new perspective of the leader is to embrace uncertainty, ambiguity, and complexity.

If complexity is a fact of life, leaders must identify opportunities within the complexity rather than running scared from it. Phil Hodgson, co-author of *Relax: It's Only Uncertainty*, observes: "The CEO faces uncertainty outside the organization in the form of expectations about organizational performance, direction and, if appropriate, stock price. But also faces uncertainty inside the organization in the form of managerial performance, operational effectiveness and realization of human potential. The role of the CEO is therefore to choose the areas of uncertainty where the strategic challenges will be met externally, and support the areas of learning where the managerial challenges will be met internally."

The new perspective of the leader is to build intangible network value.

The leader's job is to appreciate and build the intangible network values of the organization. The leader's ability to build networks inside as well as outside and the leader's ability to build trust are critical to this. "I would say that the most important aspect of the CEO's job is to act as the symbolic center of the company, both towards the internal network that is the company and towards the outside world," says the Swedish writer, businessman and media guru Alexander Bard. "The CEO personifies the image of the company, embodies the brand. And in an attentional rather than capitalist economy, this means the CEO should radiate credibility-aiming-to-create-trust rather than success-aiming-to-create-envy. This is the only way to keep both the internal networks and customer relations networks functioning smoothly in a climate of vastly increased competition in the credibility stakes. We're talking corporate contemplation centers rather than golf clubs."

The new perspective of the leader is as a talent spotter and talent attracter.

The legendary General Motors CEO Alfred P. Sloan insisted on sitting in on interviews of senior managers. Bill Gates is similarly dedicated to spotting talent. "I would have to say my best business decisions have had to do with picking people," says Gates. Gates is in many ways the ultimate intellectual capitalist having attracted and assembled an array of the best programmers. Only the best need apply – "If you have somebody who is mediocre, who just sort of gets by on the job, then we're in big trouble," says Gates who appreciates that a single programmer can change an industry. If you spot them early the commercial equivalent of alchemy occurs.

The new perspective of the leader is to shape context.

Leaders must now invest time and energy into creating context, a kind of tacit and explicit structural capital. Leaders create the context so that people want to invest themselves and their knowledge in the enterprise. Leaders must visualize how they and their organization can deliver a good personal return to each and every individual.

Successful companies such as VISA and The Body Shop are living examples of this style. Both have highly devolved decision-making processes centered on the individual companies within the group, which are given licence to create change.

You can create context in a variety of ways. Look at what Lars Kolind achieved at Oticon, the only Danish hearing aid maker to be regularly featured in the business press. Based in Copenhagen it is renowned for its innovative approach to management. Its "spaghetti structure" was instigated by Kolind after he was head-hunted to the company in 1988 and introduced some refreshingly different ideas. These included the concept of having multi-jobs, flexible working arrangements, flexible offices and an emphasis on informal communication. To make his point about getting rid of memos, the company's entrance hall was redesigned to feature a huge paper shredder which cheerfully shredded the company's paper production. In addition to these changes, employees bought 20 percent of the company's shares.

Creating context means encouraging subversion. The leader's role is more hands-off and flexible. Skandia AFS creator Jan Carendi says that the key is to hire the best and then leave them alone, do not disturb them and, most of all, do not destroy them.

Lou Gerstner's achievement at IBM has been to create a new context within the company. Under Gerstner, IBM set up a separate Internet division, and put a respected IBM senior manager at its head. In an effort to foster an Internet culture, a design office was set up in Atlanta in 1995 – dubbed the Artz Café. Cultural flourishes include a billiard table and a ping pong table which doubles as a conference table. Employees are allowed to have pets at work including dogs and an iguana. The designers were even allowed to work on Apple Macintosh computers rather than IBM PCs.

> **People are not completely resistant to change. What they are resistant to is being changed.**

"To attract the cool, younger people in the Internet business we had to break with the whole IBM culture," a director at the Atlanta site noted. "We're the only creative bone in the IBM body." Big Blue is now trying to fuse the new culture with the old. It launched an initiative called Project Springboard, and is opening "e-business integration centers" around the world.

The new leaders create a context of values – through a working environment and a culture, which nurtures and cherishes intellectual capital.

At satellite manufacturer, Hughes Space & Communications in El Segundo, California, the onus is on informality. "We've taken a new approach here," says Arian Ward, Hughes' former leader of learning and change (and now at Work Frontiers). "We're trying to avoid top management support. As a matter of fact, I've asked them not to give it."[7]

Ward believes that employees will be far more likely to embrace new ideas about intellectual capital if they are presented to them to voluntarily accept or refuse. "The whole idea," he says, "is to get people involved in this because they care about it and they are interested in it – not because management tells them to do it. People are not completely resistant to change. What they are resistant to is being changed."

With this in mind, Ward began an effort to prototype "lessons learned" databases that will be available to Hughes' various business units through groupware technology. He called it a "knowledge highway." The idea was that new processes and practices can be shared throughout the organization in a way that enables each group, if it sees merit, to customize the knowledge to its particular needs. With an accent on information technology, he attempts to create "a common environment" in which knowledge can be easily transferred and new practices adopted freely. This is the context of the networking enterprise characterized by knowledge flow and exchange.

In practice, the new environment enabled Hughes' engineers engaged in the fabrication of communications satellites, for instance, to exchange insights about technology and process that cut development time. Such knowledge exchanges could also be captured and stored to help others (inside or outside) involved in similar projects or for future reference.

By leveraging knowledge in this way, the value creating process is perpetually enhanced and intellectual capital will expand and emerge. It is about shaping a context of structural capital and then attracting human capital to this to create the multiplier effect we talked about earlier.

COMPASS LINKS
www.microsoft.com
www.make.org
www.network.org

TAKING BEARINGS
- How does your organization shape the exchange and flows of knowledge inside and outside?
- How do you as a leader shape new perspectives for knowledge navigation?
- How do you invite the future into your organization?

A KNOWLEDGE LEADER TELLS A STORY

One of the key skills of the emergent knowledge leader is that of storytelling. It is a way to visualize values as well as nourishing flows of relationships.

"At a certain level, what we do at Disney is very simple," writes Michael Eisner in his book *Work In Progress.* "We set our goals, aim for perfection, inevitably fall short, try to learn from our mistakes, and hope that our successes will continue to outnumber our failures. Above all, we tell stories, in the hope that they will entertain, inform and engage."

"Storytelling could provide a useful tool for capturing and disseminating knowledge in organizations," says David Snowden, IBM's director of the Institute of Knowledge Management for Europe and the Middle East. "Stories are already a necessary part of an organization's life. They are told around the water cooler, confidentially whispered in the elevator, distributed via email. Moreover, organizations are beginning to understand that storytelling is not an optional extra. Stories are something that already exist as an integral part of defining what that organization is, what it means to buy from it, what it means to work for it. These are the early days in understanding the use of stories in a modern business. The results, however, are sufficiently good that we now know that there are major benefits to be achieved from the use of stories and from the development of storytelling skills."[8]

I found that storytelling was the only thing that worked.

One of the best exponents of the power of storytelling is Stephen Denning, author of *The Springboard: How Storytelling Ignites Action in Knowledge-Era Organizations*.[9] Working with the World Bank he began to explore the power of storytelling. "Time after time, when faced with the task of persuading a group of managers or front-line staff in a large organization to get enthusiastic about a major change, I found that storytelling was the only thing that worked," Denning recounts. "Storytelling gets inside the minds of the individuals who collectively make up the organization and affects how they think, worry, wonder, agonize and dream about themselves and in the process create and recreate their organization. Storytelling enables the individuals in an organization to see themselves and the organization in a different light, and accordingly take decisions and change their behavior in accordance with these new perceptions, insights and identities. The attractions of narrative are obvious. Storytelling is natural and easy and entertaining and energizing. Stories help us understand complexity. Stories can enhance or change perceptions. Stories are easy to remember. Stories are inherently non-adversarial and non-hierarchical. They bypass normal defense mechanisms and engage our feelings."

In many ways storytelling is the antithesis of what managers have been trained to do for the last 100 years. It is anti-analytical. But, says Denning, this does not mean that the role of rationality and analysis in business is dead. "Storytelling doesn't replace analytical thinking," he says. "It supplements it by enabling us to imagine new perspectives and new worlds, and is ideally suited to communicating change and stimulating innovation. Abstract analysis is easier to understand when seen through the lens of a well-chosen story and can of course be used to make explicit the implications of a story."

Companies including IBM, Disney, Cap Gemini, Ernst & Young, Siemens, Aventis, and so on, are all exploring the power of story-telling. The reason, says Stephen Denning, is simple: "The CEOs of the world are all in a dilemma: they are sitting on organizations that must change, but they have great difficulty in persuading the organization to change. Change is inevitable, yet the organization is immovable. So they are desperate. They try to coercive methods but these are very unpleasant and costly. And so they wonder: is there another way? Fortunately there is."

According to an article in *Fast Company*: "Forget bullet points and slide shows. The best leaders use stories to answer three simple questions: Who am I? Who are we? Where are we going?"[10] Leaders are beginning to realize how important it is to convey to stakeholders information about the leading indicators for the future. If they can do so with numbers – audited numbers for human and structural capital – it is all the more persuasive. But what if they go beyond this with short narratives on internal tacit knowledge processes and IC supplements to annual reports which allow people to visualize the impact of knowledge on their organization?

This is supported by the leadership guru Noel Tichy of the University of Michigan Business School. "Leadership is about change. It's about taking people from where they are now to where they need to be. The best way to get people to venture into unknown terrain is to make it desirable by taking them there in their imaginations."

Leaders transform human capital into structural capital to create a springboard for the future. Executives will have to invest more and more attention on issues such as culture, values, ethos and intangibles. Instead of managers, they need to be cultivators and storytellers to capture minds. Instead of focusing on traditional historical cost accounting, the bottom-line, and competitiveness, they will need to focus on competence and talent inflow by developing the attractiveness of their organizations.

COMPASS LINKS
www.stevendenning.com

TAKING BEARINGS
- What are the dominant stories in your organization's culture?
- What numbers do you take from accounting to spice up stories?
- What is the story of the future which you tell?

Notes

1 "Beyond knowledge management," Institute for the Future, 18–20 November 1997, Aptos, CA

2 "2000 most admired knowledge leaders announced," Teleos and Work Frontiers International, 13 November 2000. The top were: John Seely Brown, chief scientist Xerox, and chief innovation officer, Robert H. Buckman, chairman, Buckman Laboratories; Jan R. Carendi, deputy chief executive officer, Skandia; Stephen Denning, program director, World Bank; C. Jackson Grayson Jr, founder American Productivity and Quality Center; Yotaro Kobayashi, chairman, Fuji Xerox; Laurence Prusack, director, Institute for Knowledge Management; Hubert Saint-Onge, senior VP of strategic capabilities, Clarica Life Insurance; John Welch, chairman and CEO GE.

3 Most Admired Knowledge Leaders Press Release, 13 November 2000

4 Pasternack, Bruce A.; Williams, Thomas D.; and Anderson, Paul F., "Beyond the cult of the CEO," *Strategy & Business*, Spring 2001

5 Barrett, Richard, "Liberating your soul," www.corptools.com

6 Follett, Mary Parker, *The New State*, Longmans, Green and Co., New York, 1918

7 Manasco, Britton, "Leading companies focus on managing and measuring intellectual capital," *Knowledge Inc.*, undated

8 Snowden, David, "Knowledge management and storytelling," MITRE Technology Program's Technology Speakers Series, June 2, 2000

9 Denning, Stephen, *The Springboard: How Storytelling Ignites Action in Knowledge-Era Organizations*, Butterworth Heinemann, Boston, London, October 2000

10 Weil, Elizabeth, "Every leader tells a story," *Fast Company*, June–July 1998

The Intellectual Wealth of Nations

The stories of our societies and of our nations are mirrors of ourselves and our organizations.

THE NEW WEALTH OF NATIONS

"Only knowledge will give us the opportunity to create a better world with a global economy in which we all will be able to share our limited resources in the best ways," says Lars Larsson of Ericsson. Former Oticon chief Lars Kolind poses a simple challenge: "Find out how nations may develop their countries into competence lands."

In the knowledge economy, the value of corporations, organizations and individuals is directly related to their intellectual capital. But spread the net little wider and you begin to understand the possibilities. Think of nations. If intangibles are important to organizations, they are also important to the productivity and competitiveness of individual nations. How can we understand the dynamics of intangibles at work on a national scale? Can corporate longitude be translated into a new perspective on national performance?

The answer is positive. It is already happening. Indeed, it was as long ago as 1986 that a voluntary pilot study was launched in Sweden to look at intangible assets. National statistics now cover all manufacturing companies with over 500 employees.[1] Then, in 1987 a group met to discuss the area of intangibles – they met on Konrad Day, 12 November, and became known as the Konrad Group. This group included Karl-Erik Sveiby who soon went on to do pioneering research for his Ph.D. and to write about customer capital, structural capital and human capital as the three categories of knowledge capital. From the Konrad Group emerged the prototyping work on intellectual capital at a corporate level at Skandia.

In 1996 Sweden announced the "Year of Innovation" and the Skandia Future Center was established. I invited Caroline Stenfelt from the University of Stockholm and some student colleagues to prototype how our work at Skandia in IC could be translated to a national stage. The first IC of Nations was born due to her pioneering work. Later she organized the Vaxholm Summit – the First

International Meeting on Visualizing and Measuring the IC of Nations in August 1998. As a result, the Swedish government adapted Skandia's Navigator to visualize its national intellectual capital. Later, countries including Israel, Holland and, in particular, Denmark, began to visualize their respective intellectual capitals.

Sweden was an interesting nation to prototype this thinking on. "Sweden appears to be a showplace for the theory of intellectual entrepreneurship," says the country's Invest in Sweden Agency, ISA.

The ISA was the first national investment organization to apply the latest knowledge of intellectual capital to assess and compare national competitiveness and performance. "Intellectual capital forms the root of a corporation – and of a nation – that supplies the nourishment for future strength and growth. A new analytical method enables these previously unevaluated resources to be assessed and compared. This can be an important tool for selecting an international location for knowledge-based companies. Sweden offers highly attractive and competitive intellectual capital assets – assets of superior value for leading edge companies," said ISA's 1999 Annual Report.

In fact, the Navigator was easily translated from the corporate to national environment. Its focuses remained intact, but covered a range of different issues:

- **Financial Focus** including per capita GDP, national debt, the mean value of the US dollar;
- **Market Focus** including tourism statistics, standards of honesty, balance of services, balance of trade, balance of trade in intellectual property;
- **Human Focus** including quality of life, average age expectancy, infant survival rate, health levels, education, level of education for immigrants, crime rate, age statistics;
- **Process Focus** including service-producing organizations, public consumption as a percentage of GDP, business leadership, information technology such as personal computers connected by LAN's, survivors in traffic accidents, employment;
- **Renewal and Development Focus** including R&D expenses as a percentage of GDP, number of genuine business start-ups, trademarks, factors important to high school students.

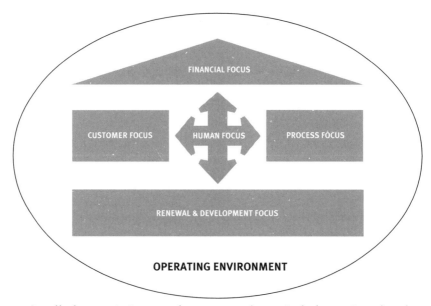

As all the statistics on the country's capital show, Sweden has embraced technology with enthusiasm. According to one survey, Sweden is the leading IT country in the world. This has not happened overnight. There has been long-term government support for technology – tax-breaks for employees buying a computer, following on from initiatives such as free Internet access for students and earlier programs to give children access to PCs. It has shaped an infrastructure and structural capital for future wealth.

The most striking IC element in Swedish management is its international networking perspective. When it comes to producing global companies, Scandinavia is remarkably successful – the only worthwhile European comparisons are with Switzerland and, perhaps, the Netherlands. Its companies transcend boundaries in ways few others can manage. Internationalization is in the Swedish genes. We are modern knowledge Vikings. Exports account for 40 percent of Sweden's GDP. In addition, Sweden has a positive trade balance in intellectual property – indeed the value generated by music royalties is equivalent to the incomes generated by Saab. Sweden also has the highest rate of musical literacy. Investment in intangibles constitute around 20 percent of GDP. According to an OECD report in October 2001, Sweden is among the leading nations in the knowledge-based economy.[2]

It is only through looking at such statistics in a holistic knowledge navigator way that they can make overall sense. Otherwise they appear to be idiosyncrasies. By looking at the IC wealth of nations rather than standard measures of national competitiveness, we gain new insights into where a country's strengths and weaknesses might lie. We can then nourish social innovation and society entrepreneurship.[3]

COMPASS LINKS
www.isa.se
www.oecd.org/publications
www.kmcluster.com
www.monday.dk
www.entovation.com
www.gkii.org
www.macroinnovation.com
www.knowledgeboard.com

TAKING BEARINGS
- What is the GDP per capita of your nation?
- What is the potential GDP per capita of your nation?
- What is the gap as a percentage?
- Which leader is in charge of bridging this gap of potential future wealth?
- What is the knowledge capital of your nation?

TAKING STOCK OF THE WORLD

Sweden is not alone. At a national level there is a great deal of activity in coming to terms with the power of intangible assets and the rise of intellectual capital.

The Dutch Central Planning Office now has a Knowledge Economy Unit. Dutch initiatives include long-term analysis of the role of knowledge in the Dutch economy as well as other work on knowledge creation in networks and the availability of human capital.[4]

The pan-European body Eurostat is taking the lead in developing statistical tools and techniques, which enable more full understanding of the knowledge economy. "The transition from the industrial to the information society is characterized by the rapid growth of intangible assets, whereas economic and social activity still relies substantially on physical, tangible goods. The relation between the two has to be defined and measured," says Eurostat.[5]

Eurostat proposes that there are four key areas around which statistics need to be gathered:[6]

Domains	Possible groups of indicators
Technology domain	Information Technology and Communications (ICT) infrastructure
	Internet infrastructure
	Digitization
	Virtualization
	Multimedia
	Internet users
	Internet penetration
Industry domain	ICT production and trade indicators
	Knowledge capital indicators
	Industry performance indicators
	Inter-enterprise alliances indicators
	New business organizational types indicators
Economy domain	Production indicators
	Economic performance indicators
	Foreign trade indicators
	Business indicators
	Deregulation indicators
	Information production and diffusion indicators
	Price and wage indicators
Social domain	Economic and social demography indicators
	Lifelong learning/training indicators
	Living standards and lifestyles indicators
	Cultural indicators
	Social inequality indicators
	Technology penetration indicators
	Internet penetration indicators
	Time use

In Israel, where the country's IC was published in 1998, a variety of alternative measures have been added to those used in Sweden.[7]

These include:

- external debt
- international events
- openness to different cultures
- language skills
- teaching effectiveness
- freedom of expression
- entrepreneurship
- risk-taking
- venture capital funds
- immigration and absorption
- women in the professional workforce
- book publishing
- museum visits
- alcohol consumption
- scientific publications.

In Denmark progress is also being rapidly made. The country has long been at the forefront of examining the role of intangibles. Copenhagen Business School's Jan Mouritsen has been working in the area for a number of years and has carried out several surveys and literature studies (the most recent of which was published in 2001).[8]

At the beginning of 1998, Denmark launched a project looking at intellectual accounting under the umbrella of its broader initiative "Ledelse, Organisation og Kompetence – LOK" which aimed to help transform Denmark from an industry to a knowledge economy. A special Competence Council was organized with Lars Kolind as chairman. This has produced interesting work on Denmark's position in the new global knowledge competition. In 2000 the Danish government also published guidelines for Intellectual Capital Statements – akin to those produced by Skandia.[9] A Danish law is now in progress to support these various initiatives.

Intellectual capital is also making an impact in the Netherlands. Its Minister of Economic Affairs recently observed: "The

Netherlands is rapidly developing into a knowledge-intensive economy … It is therefore strange that financial accounts are dominated by information on buildings and machinery, in other words the "classical" or physical production factors. The value of knowledge – the R&D work, training, intellectual property etc. – is not easy to identify in accounts. And that is in fact the reason why young knowledge-intensive businesses in particular have very great difficulty in finding external financiers."

The Dutch government's shift has been one from having an emphasis on technology to emphasizing innovation. In 1998 it published a report, "The Immeasurable Wealth of Knowledge," which found that in excess of 35 percent of Dutch national investments were of an intangible nature.

Another nation strongly transforming itself into the knowledge economy is Singapore. It has renamed its Ministry of Labor the Ministry of Manpower as well as spending decades building an impressive system of structural capital especially for IT and telecommunications. The effect on wealth is highly visible.

Examining the intellectual wealth of nations is a major advancement. But progress is being made on a number of other fronts as the true impact of the knowledge economy is beginning to be understood:

Knowledge communities and societies

"Today we're a society awash in networks, yet starved for community," says Peter Katz, author of *The New Urbanism*. True communities built around knowledge are now emerging. Many of these are web-based. In them knowledge is free flowing, restlessly criss-crossing the globe all day long. Society entrepreneurship will be even more in demand to renew societies.

Knowledge cities and harbors

Intellectual capital can also have an impact on city planning. Planners must now create the context in which knowledge workers can be at their most productive. This may bring about radical changes in the way our urban environments are conceived. Think of a harbor. Traditionally, harbors used to be for the flow of goods. But as the value of logistics has declined we have to look at the flow of knowledge. We need to create knowledge harbors. After all, closeness to water is important for knowledge workers. It is calming – all Japanese gardens have a water feature for this very reason.

Knowledge universities

These, you may think, already exist. But, in many ways, people are now effectively "dis-educated" for the future: they are not prepared for the challenges that will arise. Universities need to be re-configured to fit changing times. At the moment, future learning is not taking place in universities; it is mostly taking place outside in industry. It still takes four years to receive a Ph.D. Why? Learning needs to be accelerated. Otherwise, there is a tremendous inefficiency and opportunity cost for knowledge workers.

COMPASS LINKS
www.minez.nl
www.ll-a.fr/intangibles
www.cbs.nl
www.efs.dk/icaccounts
www.monday.dk

TAKING BEARINGS
- Where do you see your intellectual capital for future wealth?
- Whom would you like to nominate as one among the top ten society entrepreneurs of today – for shaping tomorrow?

ARRIVAL

My learnings from this journey are many. What I know is that the wave is increasing. It has gathered within it universities, accounting standards groups, political and business communities. The message is that we need to surf the wave of knowledge economics or drown.

The opportunity is great. There are a great many people who are lost at sea, lost in the fog of the labor market, the stock market or confused by the political world. They need to understand corporate longitude otherwise they will continue to go around in befuddled circles. Knowledge navigation will continue on the quest for the new wealth of nations.

There is no end, just another question, another curious leap into the dark. In the knowledge economy, the beginning is an end in itself.

Notes

1 See Statistics Sweden at www.scb.se; Stenfelt, Caroline *et al.*, "IC at national level," University of Stockholm, 1998

2 OECD Scoreboard 2001 – Towards a knowledge based economy

3 See the work of Mack M. Elroy, founder of MacroInnovation Inc.

4 See Dutch Central Planning Office at www.cpb.nl and Statistics Netherlands at www.cbs.nl

5 "EPROS – The European Plan for Research in Official Statistics," European Union 2000

6 "Statistical indicators for the new economy," Eurostat, 2000

7 "IC of Israel 1998," E. Pasher & Associates, Israel

8 Mouritsen, Jan, "IC and the capable firm," Copenhagen Business School 2001

9 Danish Ministry of Industry Guidelines for Knowledge Accounts 2001

INDEX

More power to your [business-mind]

Even at the end there's more we can learn. More that *we* can learn from your experience of this book, and more ways to add to *your* learning experience.

For who to read, what to know and where to go in the world of business, visit us at **business-minds.com**.

Here you can find out more about the people and ideas that can make you and your business more innovative and productive. Each month our e-newsletter, *Business-minds Express*, delivers an infusion of thought leadership, guru interviews, new business practice and reviews of key business resources directly to you. Subscribe for free at

▶ **www.business-minds.com/goto/newsletters**

Here you can also connect with ways of putting these ideas to work. Spreading knowledge is a great way to improve performance and enhance business relationships. If you found this book useful, then so might your colleagues or customers. If you would like to explore corporate purchases or custom editions personalised with your brand or message, then just get in touch at

▶ **www.business-minds.com/corporatesales**

We're also keen to learn from your experience of our business books – so tell us what you think of this book and what's on *your* business mind with an online reader report at business-minds.com. Together with our authors, we'd like to hear more from you and explore new ways to help make these ideas work at

▶ **www.business-minds.com/goto/feedback**

[**www.business-minds.com**
www.financialminds.com]